Patterns of Faith
Around the World

Other books by Wilfred Cantwell Smith published by Oneworld:

Related titles published by Oneworld:

Patterns of Faith

Around the World

WILFRED CANTWELL SMITH

ONEWORLD

OXFORD

PATTERNS OF FAITH AROUND THE WORLD

Oneworld Publications
(Sales and Editorial)
185 Banbury Road
Oxford OX2 7AR
England
http://www.oneworld-publications.com

Oneworld Publications
(US Marketing Office)
160 N. Washington St.
4th Floor, Boston
MA 02114

ISBN 1–85168–164–7

Cover design by Design Deluxe
Printed in England by Clays Ltd, St Ives plc

Contents

Preface

This book is a revised edition of a work that originally bore the title *The Faith of Other Men*. As is the case with everything else on earth, languages develop and change over time – slowly, or in our day rapidly; and words alter their meaning. As regards that title from years back, three issues today arise.

The first, and most conspicuous, is its use of "men," which was at that time the standard (and indeed only) counterpart English word to the term found in perhaps most other languages on earth signifying "human being," while some other, quite different, term serves those languages in the sense of "adult male human being."[1] When this work was first published, no one (for instance, none of the translators into other languages) misapprehended what was being said.[2] Nowadays many readers do, or are offended. Accordingly, in this revision the language throughout[3] has been updated.

In this task I have had the sensitive assistance of Ursula Hines, my granddaughter, and I wish to express my gratitude.

Another matter is more subtle than that "gender" issue, as it is these days generally called (another innovation). This other is equally significant. It concerns the word "other," dropped from the new title in this version. It has been dropped also, one trusts, from the worldview of us all. This book was originally constituted of a series of radio talks delivered in North America. At that time there were few exceptions to the point that Hindus, Muslims, Buddhists, Chinese, were in general, for those being addressed, people living far away, on other continents. They were strangers of whom one had heard but whom one did not know, had never met. Today, happily, this is no longer so. Not merely were traditions other than the Christian, Jewish, or secularist seen as "other." Participants in those traditions also were themselves "other;" persons that these traditions helped to shape. We all now live, and know that we live, in a pluralist context. That too has required updating. Although some may perceive those of different background from themselves as "other," certainly I myself do not, having come to feel that these women, these children, these men, these friends, are not that; they are instances of "us." They are parts of the human community that is "we."[4]

Also subtle, certainly significant, and less widely noticed, has been the shifting meaning of the English word and idea "faith." That term began to change its meaning seriously in the eighteenth century and has continued to develop since.[5] By now, for many English-speaking people it has lost the meaning that I have intended in this work. Yet after considerably pondering on whether I should not change it also, so far has the word come to connote something other than what is being pointed to here, I finally decided to retain the term in my title. Many today hear it or read it as indicating something reified and formal rather than intimate and personal. Yet what it traditionally signified has been so precious, throughout history and throughout the world, and in continuously modified form has been so central in my own perception of the world and of humanity, that I have been unwilling to acquiesce in its loss. I hope that any who read this book may recognize what is being referred to; may recover – or at least understand here – the inner human quality being adumbrated.

Some commentators have spoken of my concept of faith as if it were specifically mine, something particular, as well as differing from a (the?) nowadays current one. My contention is that it is not my idiosyncratic conception, in that it is continuous with the classical notion that in earlier centuries the leading thinkers, and presumably those who heard them, had in mind – continuous with that, even though critical of its past limitations, and admittedly revisionary. It is the traditional view modified by being enlarged, expanded to embrace more centuries, more areas of the world, more modern knowedge. It aims at rendering more "inclusive" this language also!

My hope is that the work as it unfolds will itself have clarified what is under discussion. I deem it important that we do not lose our sense of what is at issue in these outward and diverse specific matters that I am here calling various "patterns" of faith's manifestations in human life.

What faith is, even what it may best be conceived as being, are not the questions that I have intended to answer. My aspiration has been not to say what faith is but to portray how it has appeared in human life, how it has made itself evident in history.

It is easier, of course, to say what "faith" over the centuries, and in our title here, has not meant, than to affirm what it has meant and does mean. One may certainly say that faith is not something observable. It comes closer to being indefinable. One can give, presumably, an ostensive definition, pointing to situations where in some fashion it has been expressed by the human beings involved. It is, however, too deep, too broad, too rich, for any one of its expressions in human life to be more than partial, transitory – or indeed, for all of them together (thus far, at least, in history!). This partiality, this transitoriness, includes certainly attempts over the centuries and around the world to express it in words; in principle, no verbal definition can be at all adequate.[6]

Almost everything that I have published since the first edition of this present book has been an attempt to adduce instances of, and to discuss and to explore the significance of, human manifestations and expressions of faith (and thereby to make some small contribution to our fuller understanding of what it is to be human). The instances have been drawn from my study, however limited, of the cultural history of the world. I will not try to summarize these here, of course; but perhaps I may be allowed to note some nowadays popularly accepted ideas that I discern that faith is not; or at least that the word has traditionally not primarily been used to signify, and that in this book it is not intended to signify.

One modern problem shows itself in that a plural "faiths" has come into use in English, as have particularized yet gross singulars such as "the Christian faith," "the Jewish faith," "the Buddhist faith" – as if these were distinct but internally coherent forms. So far as the plural is concerned, this is as untoward as to speak of various "courages." My brother's courage has come out in ways different from mine. The courage of any one person last Tuesday morning was no doubt strikingly different from his or her courage one afternoon last month. At some times indeed we show, and perhaps have, practically no courage at all. Yet all these occasions, positive and negative, are diverse instances of a universal human quality, of which each of us has radically differing amounts and differing manifestations in differing circumstances. Yet we do not speak of these drastically varied forms that courage has taken, and takes, as distinct qualities. Different "patterns" of courage, we human beings could be said to have. Differing upbringings and cultures inculcate them; yet no one who is truly human is entirely devoid of this quality altogether – however it be expressed, and however inadequately; and however often we fail to find it in ourselves and prove unable to act in terms of it. Or at least we may say that no one who is truly human is entirely devoid of the potentiality for it. And no one human being, or group, or age, or situation, has ever displayed courage in all its range, and depth.

In traditional Christian usage "faith" denoted a universal quality; yet – paradoxically? – one definitely not worldwide (as we today know it to be), except potentially. The perception was that Christians have faith, other groups do not (some adding, "alas"). The same pertains to traditional Muslim perceptions.[7] It is one aspiration of this present book, along with others that I have written, to suggest, even to demonstrate, that traditional Christian exclusivism was wrong – but can be outgrown without abandoning the positive features of that faith.

Classically the Church, or similarly the Muslim world, was right that faith is fundamentally one, wherever it be found. They were wrong that its only form is a particular pattern with which they were familiar.

Even apart from universalism and the question of faith among "outsiders," it is absurd to speak even of "the Christian faith," given, for instance, the conspicuous historical, and present, diversity between for instance Quakers and Russian Orthodox; and given the situation these days in Northern Ireland.[8] Similarly of others: a notion of "the Hindu faith" is countered by such matters as the impressive disparity among Indian philosophers, or between them and village practices – let alone, among villages in India; and among centuries in the case of all traditions. There is no fixed pattern of belief, practice, attitude, moral teaching, vocabulary, or of anything else, to characterize what is sometimes erroneously called the Christian community or the Hindu community or the like. (It would be pleasant if all Christians had historically been or were today a true community! – rather than a collection of at times quarrelsome groups and individuals over the centuries. A "Hindu community" has not been even a Hindu idea or aspiration; let alone, a "Hindu faith." The very word "Hindu" is a foreign importation, and relatively recent.) Personal faith differs from person to person and from day to day, in depth and genuineness, in force and vividness, in expression.

Yet it is a thesis of this book that basically it is and has been more humanly universal than any of these variegated forms in which it finds outward expression.

Faith, then, like courage, like humility or pride, like love, truth, fear, cannot be observed directly. These cannot be investigated "objectively" – none of them is an object in the world; they are qualities in persons' hearts and minds. They can be suggested, by examples of occasions when, and forms through which, they have found human manifestation. Sensitive observers, being themselves human, can and regularly do move from observing the outward signs towards learning and appreciating the human quality involved in a particular case – though further occasions may provide new insights. (Hypocritical performance of superficially comparable actions, or hypocritical statements of the same propositions, may be occasions and forms for expression of the lack of the quality. Again, sensitive human observers can normally perceive the difference.)

Before closing this section, we may mention one final aspect of the changing meaning of the term "faith." For many these days the word conjures up a notion of holding certain ideas, agreeing with some proposition (such as that there is a God). This confusion, between having faith and believing, was one of the major grounds for my hesitation about retaining the word "faith" in our title.

Simply to be a theist is by no means to be a person of faith. To be a non-theist is by no means not to have faith. Belief is not faith; it is one expression of faith, at a conceptual and verbal level. Believing something, as an intellectual stance, is at a considerably lower level than the deeply personal one, of living in, and by, faith. ("Oh ye of little faith" was not addressed to those whose ideology was deficient.) Many have in our day rejected the word, and what they think of as its meaning; my retaining the word is because I have something quite else in mind. On this particular question, however, I have written two substantial books which are being published along with this one;[9] and we therefore do not pursue the matter here.

Yet people's subordination of formal manifestations of faith to faith itself and to the quality of a given manifestation has been, and continues, prominent; and consequential is a further difficulty, to which we now turn.

Conspicuous to historians – and, vividly, to secularists – is conflict between and among diverse religious groups from time to time. Instances have regularly been of a "we *versus* them" sort, not unlike "tribalism" as this is often called in other cases. Paradoxically, this is linked to the question of a sense of transcendence, which often has supported it on the one hand, and collides with it on the other.

Persons and communities of faith have regularly recognized that therein they are in touch with something,

Someone, beyond the ordinary world; something within them, around them, yet "above" them, greater than they. It exceeds their grasp, but not their reach; their comprehension, but not their apprehension. This I call "transcendence." Noticeable in the history of faith is that those involved have tended to assert that their faith derives from a transcendent source, even constitutes a human relationship with a transcendent reality. The negative side of this has underlain the attitude of some religious groups or persons that their view of the universe is absolute, indisputably right, and that any position that differs is therefore indisputably wrong and to be dismissed, if not to be crushed. Countering this, one may accept the premise but draw rather the inference that we have here been at pains to stress: that any human apprehension in the faith realm is inevitably partial, usually markedly partial and inadequate, and sometimes downright destructive.

The claim of a relationship to a transcendent source deserves to be taken seriously. Yet it has often been made without a recognition of a crucial fact: that, however absolute the other side, the human side of the relation is always inescapably finite and partial. The finitude and partiality apply to one's own apprehension, of course, and to that of one's community and one's era.[10] When there has been such a failure to recognize this finitude, this partiality, there have regularly been unhappy, not to say disastrous, consequences. Persons and groups with faith have far too often in human history lacked humility.

Yet there is irony here. For some have said that humility is one facet of faith, or one expression of faith. (I personally would be one of them.) Faith is indefinable, we affirm. It can be suggested, only; inferred only. It can be finitely evinced – in various forms, including conceptually. Involved here is a sense of that transcendent reality to

14

which faith has been said to be a relation, as well as the source from which it derives. The very fact of its being the *human* awareness of and response to that reality, and the very fact of that reality's being transcendent, together explain, and even entail, the further fact of inescapable limitation of any instances of faith here on earth. How then could it be defined? My own view would be that any appreciation of beauty; any striving for truth; any pursuit of justice; any recognition that some things are good, some are bad, and that it matters; any feeling or practice of love; any love of what theists call "God;" all these and more are examples of personal, and communal, faith. (It is hardly far-fetched to say that God is love, that God is truth, and the like. It is less often said, but if one is using theist vocabulary one can hardly avoid saying, that beauty is God, truth is God, love is God, and so on.)

Some readers of this book will be theist; others will not. For those who are, ultimate reality is summed up in the concept "God," and for them the concept "faith" is recognizable as signifying the human response, with God also its source, its sustainer, its reward, and much else, and a human relation to that Being. They will have had no deep difficulty with the word "faith" as used here, beyond perhaps for some an enlarged vision of who is involved, in how many diverse "patterns" it is to be found, and at how many levels – theoretic, practical, personal – it is expressed and nurtured.

For non-theists – notably Southern Buddhists, and in some ways most Asians and others who do not think primarily in a Western language, and some secularists – ultimate reality is regularly conceived also as transcendent. (This last is a word that I use often since it applies to both groups.) For them the concept "faith" as used here will have been less straightforward. Other Western secularists conceive it as something that they reject outright because to them it has one or more of the recently popularized meanings that I myself have been criticizing here. For them this essay will have been helpful if it enlarges understanding of fellow human beings for whom "faith" signifies something profoundly important, valuable. I have been interested to note lately that many of those moderns who reject such traditional but now disparaged terms as "faith" and "religion" have nonetheless recognized a quality in our life that they have begun to call "spiritual," or "soul," or other alternatives.[11]

For some, a helpful suggestion (not a definition! – we need hardly re-emphasize further the indefinable mystery) might be in part: that faith is sensitivity, and response, to the intangibles of ultimate worth. We recognize them all too dimly, and act, in terms even of our discerning, all too feebly. Yet as human we are not left utterly alone, to grope blindly in the dark, nor to struggle without support. We can, to some degree, perceive what is of ultimate value; and can, to some degree, allow it to shape our lives; and rejoice.

Patterns of Faith
Around the World

Part One

PATTERNS OF FAITH

Introduction

For several years I lived in Lahore, nowadays a major city in Pakistan but at that time a provincial capital of undivided India. I was on the faculty of a Christian college in the university; this means that the institution was Christian in name and in direction, and aimed at being Christian in spirit. The majority of the faculty, strikingly, were Hindus, Muslims, and Sikhs; and so were most, by far, of our students. The Christians among us were attempting to illustrate and to live out our faith; our colleagues, participants in other traditions, often reverent individuals, were doing the same with theirs. They were happy to work with us, as we with them, towards constructing and maintaining a community – a friendly and cooperative community, religiously diverse.

Such a situation meant that for each member of the college our living was set in a context of this religious diversity; living and thinking, teaching and learning. All of us, faculty, staff, and students, carried out our daily tasks and our deepest reflections in an environment in which the majority were members of other and divergent religious groups. This had implications not only for the person of firm conviction. It was interesting also for the lukewarm and the sceptical. Among the students, even the would-be atheist sophomores found themselves in a more complex and tricky position than had their counterparts at, say, the University of Toronto where I myself had been an undergraduate some years earlier. In India as in the West many of the young were rebellious and impelled to reject; yet amidst all the variety what was one to reject? In what sort of God was one to choose not to believe? Also, the political situation at that time, shortly before the splitting of British India into the new nations of India and Pakistan, kept one from drifting into any glib notion that religion is not important, that the task of building up a progressive society can be carried forward without bothering about what people believe or cherish. On the Hindu/Muslim question, as an economic and linguistic issue, and a social and political and religious one as well, Indian nationalism presently ran into flaming disaster. This – plus the fact that we were after all a missionary college – was enough to remind all of us that faith is a serious and fundamental matter, to be neither taken for granted nor dismissed, but to be wrestled with in all profundity. The problems of religious divergence presently became vivid in our group, and pressed hard.

In this matter of religious diversity, our college was, of course, typical of the city in which it stood; and indeed of India at large. I would like to suggest also that the situation is in fact representative of today's world, for all of us. Although we are coming to recognize it only slowly, in fact modern life for all humankind is more truly pictured by that situation in Lahore than it is by the sort of over-simplified religious society with which most of us have been immediately familiar. We are tempted to think of circumstances such as those that I have described as somewhat odd or remote. Instead we should realize that for this latter part of the twentieth century with its "one world," it is rather *our* background here in Western culture that is partial and unrepresentative. The religious life of humankind from now on, if it is to be lived at all, will be lived in a context of religious pluralism.

This is true for all of us: not only for "humankind" in general on an abstract level, but for you and me as individual persons. No longer are people of other persuasions peripheral or distant, the idle curiosities of travellers' tales. Increasingly, not only is our civilization's destiny affected by their actions; as well, we drink coffee with them individually.

A student in a theological college in the West finds him- or herself under the persuasive influence of a visiting Hindu swami. Resident in some relatively small towns these days is a Muslim preacher from Cairo, recently come to the mosque there. A Parsi is director of a symphony orchestra. An attractive "Buddhist church" is visited by many inquirers. A simple advertisement in a university students' daily paper brings many undergraduates together for a serious discussion group series on the Buddha's teachings, led by a Sri-Lankan-born American, or a Canadian Buddhist priest. In the nineteenth century the Christian missionary effort spread around the world. Today, in the United States, missionaries from India, Japan, and the Muslim world are to be found preaching their creeds to an inquiring generation. Parents long since became accustomed to their sons and daughters being attracted away from the ancestral faith towards "unbelief" (or for a time perhaps Marxism), but the newer thing is for them to find their children turning their attention to alternative ancient forms of faith.

I personally do not expect many conversions from one tradition to another anywhere in the world in the coming hundred years. Yet we may all confidently expect increasing encounters among the varying traditions; and consequent ferment within each group. It will become increasingly apparent, and is already essentially true, that to be a Christian in the modern world, or a Jew, or an agnostic, is to be so in a society in which others, intelligent, devout, and righteous, are Buddhists, Muslims, Hindus.

The problems that this new situation poses are not only intellectual – though they are that, and we need many good minds to work on them. The matter is equally moral, and social; and involves us all. Surely the fundamental human problem of our time is to transform our new world society into a world community.

The technological and economic aspects of this are already vigorously under way. The political aspects, which are trickier, are getting attention, though it is only very partially successful. Yet the intellectual, moral, and spiritual aspects are no less important. Those who have lost their faith, or whose faith is inadequate to humankind's new responsibilities, will not be able to build and hold the new world order without which we perish. Nor can that new world order be the work of those whose only vision is to impose their particular scheme upon everyone else. That is the mistake of many – Communists for a good while, fundamentalists of various sorts, and many others. Let us hope that even if in a subtler and less roughshod fashion it will not unwittingly be our mistake. It is a particular temptation for some types of liberal humanist or secular rationalist. Of these, many tend to believe that religious faith is a private matter or even an unimportant matter which ought not to obtrude; and assume that everyone else must agree with them, and that world cooperation can be built on this negative idea. Yet it is an idea that in fact most of the world rejects – for solid reasons.

The challenge is for us all to learn to live together with our seriously different traditions, not only in peace but in some sort of mutual trust and mutual loyalty. We sometimes forget that this means arriving at a point where outsiders can trust us, as well as one where we can understand, respect, and honor them. It means also arriving at a point – most of us are nowhere near it as yet – where we can appreciate others' values without losing our allegiance to our own. The world reaps little profit from those broad-minded relativists who accept the diversity of human loyalties because they feel that no loyalties are ultimately valid, nothing is inherently worthwhile. Modern relativism is sophisticated cynicism – and is a devastating, not a constructive, force. Intellectually, besides, it is poverty-stricken: no one has understood the diverse forms of faith of humanity if our so-called explanation of them makes fundamental nonsense of each one. That we worship God in radically different ways is a matter much too profound for glib or supercilious treatment. It poses not only an intriguing intellectual problem, but a serious political and social and moral one. Any attempt to grapple with it must do justice not only to the diversity but to the primary fact that among us most do worship God.

This new world situation, with its multicultural dimensions, involves our political leaders, our intellectuals, our trading economy, our planning engineers, and, in the end, all of us in our daily contacts. Fundamentally, I think it is hardly going too far to say that finally one must become a new type of person to live aptly in the new world community that is struggling to come to birth. This is true on the religious level as on others.

How then are we to do this? Who can help us see our way in this new adventure? The universities of the world are beginning to take up these problems at the specialist level; and there is a growing body of academic analysis and careful scholarship in this realm. Some of this is what is called "comparative religion" or "history of religion(s)," though the field is known also by a number of other designations.

In the work of such enterprises, progammes at Harvard, at the University of Tokyo, at McGill, Karachi, Chicago, more traditionally at Leiden and Paris, are collecting the data in this field of the world's religious history, analysing them, attempting to present them in intelligible fashion, and applying themselves to the intellectual task of seeing the total situation truly and providing the ideas with which we can intelligently respond.

Serious students approaching this field of study are likely to be daunted at first by the formidable range of languages involved, and the degree to which psychological, sociological, historical, and other considerations intertwine. Soon, however, they are caught up in the fascination and profundity of the exploration. Personally, I believe that the problem posed in this area is at least as important for humanity as that of nuclear physics; as intellectually challenging, as intricate, as exciting, as consequential. The forces with which these studies deal are as weighty and as explosive; the endeavor to understand them is as critical; the challenges are as new and as profound. For those of us for whom we human beings are ultimately more significant than our material environment, for whom our minds and spirits are more crucial than the things that we control, the questions are more basic than, certainly, any atomic ones.

Comparative religion as a topic of disciplined scholarly study may be considered on three levels: discovering the outward facts; learning the religious and human meaning; and drawing generalizations. I think it is important to clarify these: partly because confusion in this realm has been common, and also in order to make clear what we shall be attempting to do in this little book (and what we shall not).

The first two of these levels are both concerned with the ascertaining of data: discovering the actualities of the religious life of the various communities of humankind; in the past, and today. You might expect this to be relatively easy, but it is not so simple as one might suppose. This is why I have spoken of it as at two levels: one of external facts, one of interpretation and meaning. We must learn what precisely have been and are the doctrines, institutions, and practices, the symbols and patterns, of the world's various communities. We must further endeavor to know what these have meant to the tradition's adherents. It is one thing to know, for instance, that in Christian worship there is a cross; it is another to know what the cross means to the Christian who is worshiping. Something similar holds for other groups, other symbols, other ages. The purpose, then, is to know accurately the religious forms of a people, and to understand with imaginative sympathy the significance of these forms in the religious life of those for whom they have been avenues of faith.

A good deal of progress has been made over the past century in the former of these realms, the factual, so that we know a very great deal about the religious life and history of all humankind. Some progress is today being made in the latter realm, of appreciating faith; not much as yet, but some. There are still people who would claim that no one can really understand a religion who does not participate in the practices with sincerity, and who does not personally hold the doctrine. On the whole, however, it is beginning to be true that we can grasp just a little, at least, of how the world looks to a person whose faith is different from our own. The task is difficult and precarious, but I am convinced that it can be done. In any case, I am sure that it is worth making the attempt, and it is here that I plan to put our emphasis in this book.

For a good while now Westerners have been curious about other people's customs and beliefs, and an interest in what is called "the religions of the world" has of late been lively. A certain pattern has developed, in which the panorama of human religious life across the world is described under a series of headings: Hinduism, Buddhism, Confucianism, and the like – a number of separate systems, each one called a religion. It has been supposed that the way to understand religious life is to learn at least something about each of these various systems. You will probably be surprised to hear that I intend to challenge this approach. It would take a sizeable book to set forth my argument that this is not the best way to understand what is going on. This much can be said here: that it is possible to know a good deal about what are called the various religious systems, and still not to understand the people whose lives they help to form.

This traditional pattern is not the one that I intend to follow. My aspiration is not to get you to understand, for instance, Buddhism; but to help you to understand Buddhists. And this means, basically, trying to help you to see the world as a Buddhist sees it. Another way of expressing the same point is to say that I do not propose to talk about other people's customs and beliefs, but about other people's faith.

This is in some ways more difficult, though I think it is correspondingly more rewarding. Those of you who have been influenced by the traditional type of presentation may perhaps feel disappointed that I do not offer a brief description or even outline of the various systems.

Apart from my own conviction that this is not the quickest way to the heart of the matter, there is the further point that this type of systematic presentation is already available in a number of books, including paperbacks, so that anyone whose interest is in the systems as systems can readily find what he or she wants in a variety of easily accessible sources. Probably many of my readers have already encountered some of them.

If inner faith rather than outward system is to be our concern, then, how are we to deal with it? The method that I have adopted is this, and I am hopeful that you may find it rewarding: I will choose one characteristic item from the system of each major group, an item that may serve in some small way to represent the faith of that community; and will explore with you the meaning that that item may have for those for whom it serves as an expression of their faith. The item will be of varying sorts – an image, a phrase, a ceremony; in each case we will examine it as a symbol. In this way I hope that we shall get some inkling of how what seems to us at first unfamiliar, and even odd, may on inquiry suggest to us how other people look at the world.

The world at which they are looking is, of course, the same world that you and I observe, both tangible and transcendent, concrete and spiritual. And the people who do the looking, Chinese, Indians, of the Near East, are basically the same kinds of person as are you and I. But the ways that we in the West have looked at the universe, whether Christians, Jews, or secularists, are very special ways of our own; and our endeavor here will be to try to apprehend how others perceive the night sky, their neighbors, the making of a living, love, death, moral conflict, and all that makes human life human and lively.

The most important single matter to remember in all this is that ultimately we are dealing not with religions but with religious persons.

Our aim in these essays, then, will be, basically, to arrive at a more vivid awareness of the religious quality of the lives of these persons, who are nowadays our neighbors. We shall be highly selective, both with regard to the communities that we single out for attention, and with regard to their highly complex and elaborate systems. In each case we can choose only one facet of these for consideration. In selecting communities, we are perhaps justified if we confine our attention to the four major groups that, along with the Jews and Christians, comprise the great bulk of humankind today; namely, Hindus, Buddhists, Muslims, and Chinese. Together, these headings would cover at the present time perhaps eighty percent or so of the world's population religiously. In the matter of the inadequacy of any one symbol to portray the faith of a people, I can only plead that in these studies I have come to believe that it is preferable to explore one part in some depth than to survey a wider field more superficially. The surest way to misunderstand a great religious tradition is to miss its profundity. I trust that, in pursuit of seriousness, you will be willing to sacrifice extension of coverage – especially if we are quite explicit and self-conscious that that is what we are doing. Let me assure you now, with both candor and force, that we shall inevitably be leaving out a great deal. Any tradition that has moved hundreds of millions of persons through many centuries – won their loyalty and awe, inspired their poetry and courage, preyed upon their gullibility and excused their foibles, teased their intellects and warmed their hearts – such a tradition is not to be summarized in a few paragraphs.

My plan, then, is to deal with our subject at what I have called the second of its three levels: that of faith as it is found among the differing groups. We shall more or less neglect the first level, the sheer presentation of facts, the level of outward religious system. There remains the third level of comparative religion studies, of which we have not yet spoken. This may be called comparative religion proper: that is, the endeavor through a comparative study of all the diverse phenomena and their interpretation to induce some general truths. In view of our world's religious diversity, what can we say of human religiousness itself? One cannot study human religious life comparatively until one has something living, affective, before one to compare. After the attempt to understand the individual faiths comes the attempt to understand the fact of faith itself, in the light of its history – to understand it as a well-nigh universal human phenomenon, immensely diversified in particular, remarkably persistent in general. Once one has surveyed this vastly wide and profuse field, what emerges? Can one make any overall sense out of so bewildering a panorama of facts? In their profundity, problems of this kind are beyond the range of this book. Yet we shall come face to face with some of them towards the end of this book, when we shall be dealing with the implications for ourselves of the faith of other groups, and shall be trying to formulate our conclusions.

There remains one dimension of the whole matter in which all three levels are involved: namely, the historical. Religiously, as in other matters, history is important – indeed, massively important. Of human religiousness in general, and of each religious tradition in particular, both our own and other people's, one may ask not only what it is but what it has been. The question is large, at every level – including that of universal significance. For it turns out, on inquiry, that things were different yesterday from the way they are today. By implication one may then ask what they may become tomorrow. What may become of others' traditions, and one's own; of their faith, and of faith in general? This is a large issue, and one that transcends our capacity to handle in our limited space. I should like only to touch upon it here in a fashion typical of our approach throughout, by considering just one illustrative point.

In later chapters, our concern will be faith as it appears among others today. For each community, however, we must remember that there is a long and rich historical background; and before the present communities ever arose there were previous traditions, some of them mighty and consequential, that have since disappeared. The history of religion is bewilderingly rich; and we cannot go into it. Yet we do well at least to remind ourselves at the beginning how incredibly ancient among us is the tradition of religious faith itself. For this reminder, let me single out one facet of prehistoric religious life; namely, the burial of the dead.

At the present time every human society on earth has some formal ritual to deal ceremonially with the death of individual members. Not all practice burial. Certain groups have a tradition of ceremonial cremation, and there are one or two other alternatives. But as we go back in time we reach a point when the whole of humanity buried its dead. It is possible to trace elaborate ceremonies in a virtually unbroken line, in various parts of the earth – both among primitive groups and in the great early civilizations (conspicuously in ancient Egypt). When one goes further and further back to five, ten, twenty thousand years B.C.E., the pattern that one sees becomes less ornate. This has to do partly with questions of the survival of evidence, and partly it is because procedures themselves seem to have been less evolved; though massive and meticulous tombstones, as well as other later symbolisms, go back into neolithic times. The use of red ochre is palaeolithic; as is burying a body facing westward, and interring jewellery and weapons in a grave along with a body. These are various customs that survive widely until today. And many of the burial practices evidenced from extremely early times, and, even before the appearance of *homo sapiens*, with Neanderthalers, are fascinating in their intricate detail.

Some years ago I had the privilege of standing in the Rockefeller Museum in Jerusalem before a case in which the plaster was still wet, setting the skeleton of *Palaeoanthropus palestiniensis* or "Mount Carmel man," dating somewhere from a hundred to two hundred thousand years B.C.E. It had been found under a floor in a distinct excavated cyst, quite clearly buried. This is the earliest instance we have of human activity of a kind that today we call religious. While there is no way of knowing what went on in the minds or hearts of this man's community who took the trouble to bury him carefully, this much we can say: that present religious practices of humankind can be traced back for at least a thousand centuries in a continuous tradition.

Some observers have been quick to infer from the practice of burial a belief among the ancients in immortality. I do not find this cogent. Immortality is a somewhat sophisticated doctrine, a rather late endeavor to express in the form of ideas a human attitude to life, death, and the human spirit. In any case it is a doctrine, a belief, perhaps a metaphor. We are often a little too ready to infer that primitives were philosophers, intellectualizing their attitudes.

Even today we would be shocked if someone we knew treated the corpse of a friend without any ceremony, whatever his or her beliefs might be. I think we would be safer to take this early burial as indicating that, at the very dawn of human existence, people, in the presence of the death of their comrades, felt – or, saw; or, shall we say, experienced – something more profound than the animal world for a hundred million years earlier had ever experienced. And having seen it, we have never forgotten it, through all our long history since. Each of us, anew each generation, and throughout the world, repeats and continues this until today.

This much at least we may say: that prehistoric burial shows that men and women from the very earliest traces of their beginnings have recognized that there is more to human life than meets the eye, that our total significance is not exhausted within the six feet of space or sixty years of time whereby we each play our part on the stage of earth. The sober observation of the historian now agrees with the insight of the philosopher, and the faith of the saint, that human beings are not human until they have recognized that the proper response to death is poetry, not prose.

Hindus

In introducing this series of essays, I said that we would look in turn at each of the great religious traditions and would try to see something of their religious quality, not by endeavoring to present in each case the whole system, even in its main outlines – with inescapable superficiality – but rather by singling out one item in the system, to see whether we could interpret that one element meaningfully, so as to catch the flavor of the orientation that it represents. Not Hinduism, therefore, but the Hindus, as seen through one of their symbols: this will be our concern here.

You might imagine that the value of such a method would turn in part on my success in selecting a truly representative element, one that is typical of the community's attitude at large. Clearly there is something in this point, and in fact in subsequent chapters – on Buddhists, and then Muslims, and so on – I shall be trying to meet this requirement, choosing in each case for our exploration a facet of the tradition that is in some sense central, typifying the whole. We may learn something, however, from the fact that in this very first presentation we come upon what is, indeed, one of the first lessons one must learn; namely, that the various religious traditions of the world differ not only in content but in form; not only in the answers they give, but in the questions they ask. One has begun to understand the religious life of India only when one has recognized that on principle nothing can be typically Hindu. The sprawling variety is deliberate and serious. There is no system to which something can be central. And Hindus have felt there should not be. A persistent affirmation in India has been that there are as many facets of the truth as there are persons to perceive it.

The Hindu is taken aback at any suggestion that religious life should optimally be of a single pattern; that there is even in heaven an ideal to which all our minds or hearts or wills ought to conform. At the very least, intellectuals among them will be expected to choose one sort of path; more emotional or devotional types, another; and moralists and activists still another. No one item that we may choose, therefore, will be typical of the Hindu community at large. Each symbol represents, at most, one group among others.

By considering any aspect of the Hindu complex, therefore, we should be considering some Hindus and omitting many, many others. I do not propose to try to circumvent this in any way, or to deplore it, or even to apologize about it. This very point is part of the truth of the total community. One has understood India's religious life better, not less, if one accepts cheerfully its bewildering variety.

We should not be restlessly in search, then, of elusive generalizations in a realm where truth lies rather in particularities. The outside observer must learn to rejoice with the Hindus in the variety, or at least to understand the rejoicing of those to whom unity lies in God, not in something that the Westerner calls Hinduism.

There is the further point that sophisticated Hindus have tended to hold that the great mass of customs and beliefs, gods and temples, and all, that make up what others call the Hindu religion (or for that matter, the "religions" of other groups also) are but one stage on an ultimate human journey that leads beyond these things. We should be stopping short of serious Hindu affirmation, therefore, if we paused at the level of the vast Hindu religious complex. I am going to leave all that aside, then, and deal rather with one part of one of the ways (there are several) by which a Hindu escapes from "Hinduism" and moves beyond it into salvation. Hindus are free to choose. I follow them, not by describing to you what they choose from, which is vast; but by interpreting to you one item that one or another may perhaps have chosen.

I am being, therefore, selective, though not arbitrary, when I choose as our emblem a phrase, one that has been important and can be illuminating. It is a statement, and pertains to the life of the intellectual person of faith. This lends itself to our discussion and analysis here; perhaps more readily (for the moment, anyway) than would the orientations of devout and fervent *Bhakti* worshipers, or the serenity of the detached activist, or the ritual of the humble villager, all of whom and many others we regretfully, but significantly, leave out of consideration.

The phrase that I have chosen consists of three Sanskrit words, generally regarded in India as the most important sentence that that country has ever pronounced; the succinct formulation of a profound and ultimate truth about humanity and the universe. The phrase is: *tat tvam asi. Tat* means "that;" *tvam* means "thou;" and *asi* is the second person singular of the verb "to be." "That thou art;" *tat tvam asi.* It means, thou art that reality, thou art what Westerners would call God. The same truth is expressed in other ways; for instance, in the famous equation "*atman* equals *Brahman*" – or the soul of each person is God; or is the Ultimate Reality, with a large capital "U" and capital "R;" the really real. The individual self is the world soul. The human soul equals the ultimate of the universe. "Thou," or to use our more colloquial term, "you" (each one of you reading this book) are in some final, cosmic sense the total and transcendent truth that underlies all being, *Brahman,* which precedes and transcends God Himself/Herself, the Infinite and Absolute Reality beyond all phenomena, beyond all apprehension and beyond all form.

I have chosen this phrase partly because it has been so important in India. Certainly it has been historically consequential, reverberatingly so. It has been profoundly meaningful to generation after generation of brilliant intellects, many of whom have written great commentaries on it, and to century after century of consecrated personalities. For such thinkers the assertion *tat tvam asi* has been a saving truth: not only convincing, but liberating; not only true, but powerful. Earthly temptations fall away. The fetters of sin and desire and ignorance are gone, mortality dissolves, in the vision that these words express.

So we are told. But I have chosen it also just because to us in the West, with our radically different intellectual and theological background, it sounds so strange. What on earth does this phrase mean? What ever do we mean when we say, as we may say all too glibly, that certain Hindus believe this? I personally have long felt that we must be on our guard against listing a series of propositions that we say other people believe, and imagining that thereby we know their religion. We do not know what we are saying, and we would do better to keep quiet, until we grasp, at least in part, what they mean when they utter this phrase, and what it means to them. Unless we know and can feel and see what the universe looks like to someone who genuinely holds this view, then we have not understood that person, and we do not know his or her faith. What does it feel like to hold *tat tvam asi*? If we can authentically answer that question, we shall have gone a long way towards understanding one facet, at least, of Hindu religious life.

Tat tvam asi, "That thou art." These three words are
the expression, manifestly, of a profound religious experience, and have been for many, in turn, the ground of a
profound religious experience. The first point for us to
seize is that, however strange the affirmation may sound
to us initially, it is not silly. *Tat tvam asi* has been affirmed
by persons of outstanding intelligence, certainly; by persons of greatness and courage. Also, and this is at least
equally important, by persons of genuine sincerity.
Beginners are often in danger of supposing that Hindus
believe such-and-such because it is part of Hindu doctrine;
instead of recognizing, rather, that it has become part of
Hindu doctrine because Hindus believe it, because this is
their actual assessment of the world, careful, sincere, and
accurate. The same applies, of course, to Buddhists,
Muslims, and for that matter to Christians and Jews –
though this principle applies rather less cogently perhaps
in a dogmatic tradition, where participants are asked to
believe on authority. *Tat tvam asi* was originally formulated because some perceptive and outstanding religious
person wrestled with the problems of life and thought,
and finally came up with this report of how he or she saw
the universe. It has persisted now for twenty-some centuries and has been cherished, because others, too, have
tested it, and found it satisfying – something by which one
could live, and die. To see human beings and the universe
in these terms, they have testified, is deeply rewarding,
and also is self-authenticating. It is not easy to grasp what
these words mean, they say, but it is worth the struggle; is
worth all struggle. For once you have seen it, they report,
all else falls into place and you recognize that here indeed
is the final serenity, the final and solemn vision, beyond
which nothing more is needed or desired.

Of course there is no particular reason why you and I should agree with those who say *tat tvam asi*. All I am arguing at the moment is that we should take them seriously. Indeed for the moment I am not suggesting that we should concern ourselves with whether or not the proposition is valid. Our business – and this is exacting enough – is simply to see whether or not we can contrive to understand it.

Perhaps after this introduction you will be disappointed when I admit, and yet it is high time that I do admit, that I myself do not adequately understand the phrase. Let me hasten to add that this is not, I think, as preposterous as it may sound. In fact, there would be something wrong in the situation if I did fully understand it, or even if I thought that I did. For Hindus to whom this particular tradition is significant have held emphatically that the meaning of this phrase, seemingly so simple, is in fact exceedingly difficult; that only after long and arduous discipline does one gradually come, and that exceptionally, to apprehend its truth. Finally to understand it, they affirm, is to be saved.

Now to be quite frank, I am not saved, in this Hindu sense: "liberated" is a better translation of their term, freed from all the burdens and curtailments of finite existence. No, I have not fully understood what they mean. And yet I am bold enough to talk about it because I have, I think, begun to understand.

If I admit that I have not fully understood it, you may ask, then how do I know that there is something there to understand? The answer here is, first, that many Hindus of intelligence and dignity, including my friends, find it profound and serious. Secondly, I myself keep finding more in it, as I go on exploring it – or more precisely, as I go on exploring the universe and human history, with, in part, this concept in mind. Even an outsider can recognize that here indeed is one of those insights into transcendence, and into human destiny, that offers those who take it seriously increasing richness, and subtlety and an increasing numinous awareness. I said a moment ago that there would be something wrong if I did fully understand. For this truth is a mystery – not in the philistine sense that it mystifies and baffles, but, on the contrary, in the religious sense that it illuminates, but progressively and always expansively; that as one handles it, there opens up before one facet after facet of previously unsuspected wisdom, and at the same time new depths of previously unsuspected, and as yet unplumbed, uncertainty – a continuing sense that there is still more and more to be explored. I do not fully understand it: this is an understatement. Let me say, rather more frankly, that I do not much understand it. Yet I rather suspect that even Hindus, though many see in it vastly more than I do, do not fully understand it either, and that this is part of what they mean when they say that it is a cosmic truth. Any proposition that is fully understood by the human mind, and is in that sense subordinate, must be a finite truth, not a religious one. Of a religious truth, one asks only that it prove itself true in so far as one has explored it, and that it constantly beckons one on to explore it further.

There is another problem here, however, which we must face. I see something in this *tat tvam asi* affirmation, all right; an increasing something as I go along. Yet it is still little enough, goodness knows; and it is what *I* see in it – or better, it is what I see in life by means of it. How can I be sure that I am on the right track, then? How can I know that what it means to me is, so far as it goes, in the direction of what it means to Hindus? The important thing to recognize here is that I cannot be sure. Hindus understand this symbol as a religious truth, and I think that I am beginning to understand it in the same way, as therefore indeed greater than, and beyond anyone's ability to understand more than partially. I think the possibility of misunderstanding is seldom given as much weight as it deserves, whenever anyone attempts to interpret a form of faith, especially a form other than their own.

We can all understand this more forcefully if we reflect on the attempts of outsiders to understand our faith (or our lack of faith).

How many Hindus or Muslims or even Jewish friends, understand what Christians have meant in saying "in Christ we find God revealed, and in Him we find the power to live and to love"? How many Jews feel that Christians, for all the study and contact, understand their Jewish faith? Interreligious understanding is a new field of endeavor, still at a tentative and exploratory stage.

Yet, having warned you of these hesitations, I am going to do my best. I am going to try to convey, in a few words, something of what I have come to understand of *tat tvam asi*. If I succeed in enabling readers to understand, in part, what I see here, and if I have succeeded in understanding, in part, what some Hindus see, then our exploratory endeavor will have been worthwhile.

I propose, first of all, to take four areas of human life, and to tell how I see this equation applying in each area: namely, the intellectual, the aesthetic, the moral, and the area of historical development and creativity.

First, in the sphere of intellectual truth. Every teacher, every parent, knows that there are two aspects of, say, a child's acquiring new truth; let us call them sincerity, and validity. Sincerity is obviously quite fundamental; without it there is no education. To learn by rote is not really to learn at all. There is no point in children repeating parrot-like a proposition that they have been taught, if they do so coldly and mechanically, without understanding, without having appropriated it to themselves. It is really a form of cheating if children score marks in an examination by reproducing an answer that may externally be correct, but that they themselves do not believe or do not understand. We call a person a liar if, and only if, he or she says what he or she believes to be false. Certainly in any personal sense, there cannot be intellectual truth unless the person who intellectualizes appropriates the truth and assimilates it, interiorizes it in full sincerity. Surely each one of us must strive for full intellectual integrity in our intellectual life.

At the same time, however, we must strive, equally and utterly, for full objective validity. If a proposition is of no value to us unless we make it our own, also it is of no value to us unless it is externally true; unless it matches the actual facts of the outside world. We may escape being liars by being gullible to our own deceptions, but we shall not escape being fools. The utmost rigor of external accuracy, the utmost rigor of internal sincerity, combine to lead us to truth. I do not know whether you agree with me that only this combination can get one anywhere in science. I hope that you will agree that in all personal life, including religious life, the combination is where truth lies.

Certainly our goal is, must be, that we should say, whether to our neighbors or to ourselves, only what we genuinely and deeply believe, and that we should believe only what is actually true. Subjective honesty, objective validity – in so far as you achieve these, intellectually you are saved. *Tat tvam asi.*

Next, let us take the life of art. Here, what a foul bog of insincerity must be cleaned away before there can be any hope of beauty in our lives! What a lot of people, it has been remarked, will say that Milton's *Paradise Lost* is a great poem who have never read his work, or if they have read it have been bored. Modern life is subject to enormous pressures towards aesthetic insincerity, from the disc jockey to the classroom, from the art gallery to the billboard, all pushing us to accept as valuable not what we ourselves come to value, but what others praise; pushing us away, that is, from all true aesthetic awareness. I am lost to beauty except in what is beautiful to me – genuinely, sincerely. Surely we must train our children not to believe that X is beautiful, but to see that it is; to appreciate it, deeply and inwardly, truly and personally.

In modern times, this side of the argument is more readily accepted than the other, which has rather gone out of fashion, but in my view is equally fundamental; namely, that I aspire not only to see things as beautiful myself, but also to see as beautiful what is beautiful, really, and only that. There is no point in my children growing up believing that Mozart's music is better than the raucous rampage of a commercial jingle, as I maintain, if they are merely repeat-ing this on my authority, or in order to gain prestige, and do not feel it in their bones when they hear the two. They must learn to be sincere, utterly and relentlessly, in their musical as in their other judgments. Yet neither is there any point in their growing up to be sincere, if in fact they come to prefer the jig-jag assault of ephemera to the music of Mozart. For then they would be wrong. I want them to know that Mozart is better, provided that indeed I am right in holding that he is better, because they themselves have come to see that he is, because they can themselves hear the greater beauty that is in fact, objectively, there. My goal is to recognize as lovely what is in fact lovely, without deceiving myself and without being deceived – once again to combine integrity and validity, subjective judgment with objective truth.

As I say, nowadays this position is less widely held, since many people have lost their faith that beauty is objectively given, in addition to being subjectively sensed. This does not invalidate my argument, but in fact clarifies it, if you recognize that this is, indeed, a loss of faith. Those who deny the objective or absolute reference in aesthetics are rejecting the transcendent or divine quality of beauty, are failing to see it as something more than mundane. Those, on the other hand, who worship a god of beauty will quickly see the point; as will those who, being monotheist, see the God of beauty as being finally identical with the God of justice, or truth, or love, so that in our awareness of beauty, we are reaching out to touch the hem of His/Her/Its garment. Those of you who do not see beauty as absolute, and do not hold that humanity's aesthetic judgments are right or wrong in ultimately the same sense as our judgments of mundane fact, will perhaps be the first to recognize that the absolutist position I am putting forward is, indeed, a religious affirmation. This is really all that I am asking you to see.

I personally am persuaded that some things are in fact more beautiful than others, and that my task is to discover which is which, in genuine appreciation – my task, and my salvation. For those who share this conviction, this faith, one's soul is saved, musically speaking, when one can within oneself actually see and hear, in deep personal response, the excellence of such music as is objectively excellent. Your goal is to attain an inner appreciation of an outer reality; a personal sense of an impersonal truth; to appropriate as your own a cosmic quality. Ideally, *tat tvam asi*. Ultimately, you and It must coincide.

Turning now to morality, we need not belabor the discussion since the point is similar and is clear. Some things are right, some are wrong, and it matters. We must do what is inherently right. Also, however, only that person is moral who is sincere and honest. The person is not honest who deliberately does what he or she knows to be wrong; but also, those are not good people who act on what they believe yet in fact believe wrongly – fanatics can be sincere while doing a great deal of damage. Often enough the road to Hell is indeed paved with good intentions.

Finally, the same applies in creation. The artist, the stateswoman, the theologian, the bricklayer, must construct in conformity with inner standards and with outer. United States', or British, or Canadian, foreign policy is perverse, except in so far as it can combine being authentically American/British/Canadian with being truly apt to the outside situation. To the degree that it is a matter of promoting interests, no policy is finally legitimate unless it serves the interests both of the country advancing it and of the country or countries affected. (No wonder that so much foreign policy in today's competitive world is in fact immoral.) The whole of evolution is sound or awry, in so far as its inner *élan vital* is or is not both genuine and authentic, both spontaneous and appropriate.

So much, then, for this argument. This presents part of what I see in this famous phrase.

Turning to a more theological concern, there are elements in Christian and Jewish doctrine that from quite another angle may help members of those groups to see the point of the Hindu formulation. Take, for example, the biblical principle of *imago Dei*, the image of God: that humankind has been created in the likeness of God. This is a doctrine that is crucial, profound, and of inexhaustible moment. Or take the Christian doctrine of incarnation, which involves the discernment that God is truly known in human form, who represents "true" humanity. Admittedly in the Christian tradition there is also the doctrine of sin, carried in Calvin's case to a doctrine of total depravity; but even this can perhaps be seen as another way of saying what the Hindu is saying in *tat tvam asi*. For the Hindus certainly assert that this truth is a hidden, final truth, not an overt, immediate one. A person's true self, they hold, is divinity. But the person's empirical self, his or her actual mundane personality, is part of *maya*, the distracting, illusionary realm of phenomena, that obscures from mortal eyes the transcendent truth beyond. You must overcome your empirical self and realize a cosmic universal beyond it. "Not I, but Christ that liveth in me," as St. Paul put it.

Again, let me say that I may be wrong, but I see a parallel between the Christian doctrine of human sin and depravity and this Hindu doctrine of humankind's essential divinity as contrasted with existential humanity. I also allow myself, however, to speculate about another possible parallel, at first blush equally paradoxical. Christians affirm that God is personal, and give great weight to this major affirmation. Hindus affirm that *Brahman* is impersonal. It would take us too far afield to explore what they mean when they say that (or what Christians mean when we say the other). I think that both mean something rather special.[12] In any case, the Christian affirmation that God is personal bears, I believe, some relation to, and may help us to see at least part of the point of, their concomitant faith *tat tvam asi*.

There are facets in all this that could be discussed at enormous length. Please do not let me close having given an impression that I have tried to satisfy you on this issue. I shall have succeeded in my effort if I have helped us to see the sentence *tat tvam asi* as a religious symbol, meaningful to human beings and one that can repay serious attention.

Buddhists

In this book I am selecting from each religious community, in order to interpret its faith, a single symbol, in the hopes that through it we may gain an insight into the religious life of those for whom it is meaningful.

For the Buddhists, I have chosen a ceremony, and I will try to present it as it is enacted in a Burmese village. We will then see if we can uncover at least part of what it means to those involved.

Burma has long been a Buddhist country, and every village has its monastery – or temple or shrine: it is a little difficult to know what to call it, since any of our Western terms can be a trifle misleading. It is a Buddhist center, "set in a bamboo grove, flanked by shady mango trees," in a characteristic architectural form, with a seven-roofed apex. It is usually just outside the village proper, not too close, not too far away: far enough to symbolize its quality of sanctity, representing an order of life different from the day-to-day routine of the people, set just apart from it, and yet near enough to be relevant, concerned with the people's problems. Coming and going between the village and the monastery are easy and natural but are not unconscious. Between the recognized norm and the actuality of everyday life, between the abiding and the transient, the sacred and the profane, the relation is close, yet the two are not identical. They are not two different worlds, but two aspects of the life of humankind. The monastery is the village school (and literacy in Burma for both men and women has for almost a thousand years been remarkably high); it is the village dispensary, social center, retreat, old people's home, counseling service, as well as moral and spiritual focus. In the building or just nearby will be found a statue of the Buddha, the unruffled calm of which has portrayed and promoted the serenity of the monks' traditionally somewhat withdrawn but dedicated life of service.

The ceremony that I wish to present is what may be called an initiation or confirmation rite for boys, at puberty or earlier. There is a corresponding rite for girls, but I personally am not familiar with that, and we shall consider only the one. It (the boys' rite) is called *Shin Byu*. In broad sweep it compares to "joining the Church" or First Communion or Confirmation in the Christian pattern, *Bar Mitzvah* in the Jewish, and to related ceremonies throughout the world. But let us see the particularity of the Burmese Buddhist practice.

In essentials it is a re-enactment of the Going Out ceremony of the life of Gautama the Buddha. Most readers will know that story: how Siddhartha Gautama, who was later to become the Enlightened One, the Buddha, was born the son of a king and grew up in a palace, surrounded with opulent luxury, living in secure ease with the warm affection of his parents and the admiring service of all his associates. His father, the *raja*, having heard it foretold that this child might forsake the world to become a hermit, and finally a great religious teacher and saint, sought to forestall this by protecting him from all knowledge of misery and all contact with pain, and gave strict orders that his son should know only the delights of life. Gautama grew up and matured, and in due course he was married to a lovely princess, and presently they were blessed with a charming baby son. All was going exceedingly well: here was a young man, well favored and well established, seemingly with everything that a human heart could desire. But then, of a sudden, as he was being driven in his chariot through the park, the prince, by misadventure, met a broken old man, then a beggar, next a sick man, and finally a corpse; and his charioteer, on being questioned, explained to him these phenomena of decrepit old age, destitution, sickness, and death, and further explained that yes, all human beings are subject to these ills. Gautama was profoundly troubled in spirit, and went home pondering. The ills of humankind, of which he had now become aware, preyed on his mind; till eventually one night – and this part of the tale is told with vivid artistry, throughout the Buddhist world, in story and in picture – he got up, took one last loving look at his sleeping wife and beloved child, and went out – out into the world in search of an answer to human sorrow.

This Going Out, or The Great Renunciation as it is also called, is the prototype for our Burmese village ceremony, which commemorates this act by which Siddhartha Gautama went out from palace and home, wife and family, wealth and contentment, and, turning his back on these mundane satisfactions, set forth on his spiritual quest, to seek out a remedy for humanity's ills. The rest of the story, presupposed, is of course also relevant; that he not only sought but found – found the answer to all our questioning and all our need; to become, in Buddhist eyes, the Savior of the world.

In the *Shin Byu* ceremony in Burma, then, this well-known and well-loved scene has been re-enacted over the centuries, with the young village boy playing the role of the hero. It is a gala day, the whole village colorful and boisterous in festive mood and gay attire. The child is fitted out in princely garb, his family and friends feast his coming of age, rejoicing, and then at a certain point in the ceremony the child bids farewell to his family, takes off his gorgeous clothes, to replace them with the saffron robe of the monks' order, and is led away from the village to the monastery, where he is received as an inmate. He then lives in the monastery, for a length of time that is altogether unfixed. Some boys stay for only a token period of a few weeks, others remain for some years, as, in effect, boarders in a residential school as well as novices in a monastery, while a few may remain for the rest of their lives, having taken up the monastic life as their own. This, then, is the ceremony.

We have called it "a symbol," since it is a religious ceremony. Within the pattern there is a meaning, a deep and intangible significance that is symbolized; beyond the forms there is substance, or the intimation of a transcending, limitless truth. This infinite becomes in part available to us within the finite, through these finite channels that a society inherits and cherishes, and uses to express its faith and to nourish it. Can we learn something of that faith, and appreciate in part that inner meaning, by exploring the significance of these outward forms? This, we have said, is the task of comparative religion: not only to ascertain the institutions, beliefs, and practices of a tradition but to ascertain also, if one can, what these things mean to those who participate in them. Religious truth lies not in symbols but in what is symbolized – if only we can apprehend it.

Two preliminary observations are in order. The first is that of course we cannot apprehend it fully. Not only can the outsider never grasp in its entirety what a tradition means to those within it, but even those within, as we suggested in our last chapter, never apprehend fully. This is altogether proper, since, after all, religious symbols symbolize the infinite, or at the very least symbolize what is greater than we. The whole point of any religious tradition lies in the fact that it introduces us to what is greater than we and greater than itself.

Our second observation is that this ceremony, and indeed any Buddhist symbol, and indeed every religious symbol in whatever tradition, can mean different things, at different levels, to various persons – and here, to various boys (and to their parents and friends). There is more behind our own tradition, and behind other people's, than any one person can grasp. Meaning is determined in part for each participant by his or her particular experience, and by his or her capacity, sensitivity, imagination, intensity, and whimsy. We can generalize, but we should remember that that is what we are doing. The *Shin Byu* ceremony in Burma would be different from every other religious ceremony in our own or any other tradition if it could not mean somewhat different things to different people. All interpretation, then, must be suggestive rather than conclusive.

Having said these two cautionary things, however, we can go on in an attempt to interpret. Indeed in part this is fairly easy to do. For any of us, particularly if we have religious faith ourselves, even if it be of another variety, can fairly readily appreciate something, at least, of what is here involved. With only a minimum of imagination we can transpose elements so as to grasp the human significance.

From the point of view of the parents, for instance: as with any comparable rite, here the parents are participating in that profoundly moving experience of dramatically expressing their handing over of their son from their own personal charge to that of the society, and in a sense handing him over to his own charge, to be responsible now for himself. They are enacting the transition by which he becomes (that word is so disarmingly simple!) no longer the child of Buddhists, which is one thing, profoundly meaningful, but a Buddhist, which is another, equally profound in meaning. Yet the ceremony symbolizes also that their son is not only leaving their care to enter a new phase, of his own responsibility, but is doing so under the same overarching pattern as has been their own. The child identifies himself in relation to the Buddha, the Eternally Wise One, as they themselves have long since done; and subordinates himself to the traditional norms of their society, crystallized in the monastery, as they themselves have long since done. It would be a very different wrench for those parents if their child were seen as, even symbolically, leaving their care to set out to lead an independent career on his own, unrelatedly acting in unguided new directions. Instead, they see him as humanly independent, yet oriented in what they regard as the cosmically right direction, free of their control but accepting as they have done in free commitment the guidance of a transcending wisdom.

A religious tradition formulates, of course, into a pattern whatever those within it have valued, have found worth pursuing, worth knowing, worth admiring. And it is a thrilling and solemn moment to see a son cut the ties that relate him directly to his parents and at the same time turn his face in the direction that those parents have found to be supremely good. For those parents there may well be, or even must be, an inner hope that the child will discover and realize values within or through the cherished order that one has oneself missed, either to perceive or to attain. But one's knowledge that such values are there, of wisdom, comfort, joy, and truth, in inexhaustible measure, means that one rejoices to see the child set out in quest of them.

As for the boy himself, I will not try to speculate as to what goes on in his mind, at either the conscious or unconscious level. How much he personally has been moved, in his home or at previous village ceremonies, by the stories of the Buddha; how sensitive he has been, in such contacts with the monastery or with the monks as he has had, to the numinous quality of life, crystallized in these sanctities – such things will vary, of course, from boy to boy. How deep an impression the day will make on him; how seriously he takes the moment when he doffs the splendid gala attire, to take on instead the austere garb of the monastery; how touched he may be with some spiritual overtones or simply with nostalgia or mischief, as he says goodbye to his parents and sets his face towards the monastery – I leave you to judge. His later development, year by year, as it unfolds or as he unfolds it, will determine of course in part whether he gradually lets slide or minimizes or even forgets these matters, or alternatively, perhaps, spends his life slowly exploring them, to discover step by step the increasing richness and depth of the spiritual life and little by little the profounder meanings behind the symbols.

If he becomes, for instance, in modern times, a medical doctor, having gone off for his education to the big city and even perhaps abroad; or if he becomes a modern-type professional social worker, or whatever it may be, then who of us can tell how far the motivation for his career, and the constancy and integrity and devotion with which he pursues it, may be influenced by his experience at this ceremony – or by having grown up in a village and in a home where such a ceremony is traditional?

Yet we ourselves, I would suggest, even without being Buddhist, can discern and consider together briefly two at least of the major connotations of this ritual.

One of these raises a question of what one means by speaking of the truth or otherwise of a particular religious orientation. The *Shin Byu* ceremony itself, as acted out in a modern Burmese village, is of course a ceremony, a rite. It is not in itself true or false. Yet it represents something; and one can perhaps ask how far the something that it represents is true or otherwise. One can also ask how truly the ceremony represents it. And that, presumably, turns on the quality of those taking part, how seriously and competently and devoutly they do so, and the like; and with what sincerity. I have long thought that one should not speak of a religion's being true or false simply, but rather of its becoming true or false as each participant appropriates it to himself and lives it out. It is much too glib to say that "Christianity," for instance, is true (or, indeed, is false) without recognizing that my Christianity – or as I prefer to say, rather than using that gross and misleading generalization, my Christianness – may be more false than my neighbor's, or that so-and-so's may be truer today than it was last Tuesday. I believe that this point is of much greater seriousness than we usually recognize: and for our present purposes we should note in passing that the "Buddhism" of one village in Burma is truer in a particular celebration of the *Shin Byu* ceremony of one year than it is in another, or than in another village.

Yet beyond this there is a second question, which some people would call a prior question (though I am not sure

about that), as to whether that which is being represented
is, in principle, true.

What about the Going Out episode itself, then, as an
event in the life of Siddhartha Gautama? If we ask
whether this is true, there are again several levels. At the
level of prose and of history, modern scholarship is as
usual sceptical but uncertain. Probably there was an actual historical figure of this name, about the sixth century
B.C.E., quite possibly he was a prince, in at least a petty
kingdom, and it is not at all unlikely that, as was a custom
in India at that time, he left home in search of spiritual
wisdom. The details of his life are so mingled with legend
in the accounts that have come down to us that the sceptic cannot separate the two, and is left with an apparently
commanding personality, about whom we know for certain the immense impact of his faith and teaching on his
followers, but do not know for certain any specific details
of his career. This is one reason why I said just now that I
am not sure that there is here a prior question. The details
of this actual ceremony are perhaps on the same sort of
plane, so far as prosaic historical truth is concerned, as are
those of Christians' celebration of Christmas. In both
cases I personally would be concerned rather with the
poetic than with the prosaic truth. The shepherds and the
star can be made spiritually true today (or sometimes,
spiritually false), quite regardless of their factual truth in
4 B.C.E. Similarly, I think, this is so with the Buddha.

I would suggest, then, that in the Going Out myth
there is, in fact, truth; a psychological truth of almost universal validity – and that one need not be a Buddhist to see
this. The transition of the Buddha from the protected
innocence of the home, with, in his case, its particularly
high degree of ease and security and comfort, to the

painful realities of adult life, is psychologically true for us all, is it not? And this is so not merely for those born in palaces. At some point in the life of all of us there comes an awareness of old age and poverty and sickness and death; of human suffering. To some it comes earlier than to others, to some more dramatically and all at once than to others. We all, however, discover at some time in a serious, personal, realistic fashion that we and our friends are liable, indeed inescapably so, to these ills. And do not all of us parents try to shield our children, at least at the first, from this sorrow? At the very first, of course, they are shielded by their own immaturity, children's inherent incapacity to grasp what is happening, even if decrepitude and illness and death occur right beside them. Later, we as parents give them what comfort and what happiness we can; little enough, perhaps, but we do protect them, with greater or less success, against the onslaughts of a tough world. We ourselves were protected for a time in our parents' home; but since then we have come out of that security and ease into the realities of maturity.

There is, then, as I see it, in universal human terms, a psychological, and indeed a philosophic, truth in this Buddhist ceremony; a truth that Burmese villagers do well to re-enact and to re-ponder.

My second point, however, would go further: that there is in universal human terms a moral and spiritual truth here, too. The renunciation of wordly values, in favor of wisdom and spiritual perception: this also, surely, is common in some form to all moral and religious life. Each one of us can set out in quest of moral values and spiritual goals, only if we renounce the immediate mundane rewards of morally bankrupt and spiritually unenlightened existence, in some fashion, at some point, with more or less conscious, if not more or less sudden, volition and decisiveness. And the more dramatically, the more forcefully a growing child learns this lesson, the better. Again this particular representation over-dramatizes, perhaps, over-sharpens the contrast. I personally have been struck and even troubled, I will confess, that the price paid by Gautama included leaving his family, as though wife and child were a drawback instead of a help in spiritual and moral life. Yet those among us who are fortunate in this regard, and are Christian, must not complacently forget that Christ also made the same point, in a comparably radical, if not an overly strident, way: "If anyone comes to me and does not hate his own father and mother and wife and children and brothers and sisters, . . . he cannot be my disciple."[13] To opt for truth and goodness is a decision that must involve a willingness, at least, to surrender, if need be, everything else – everything.

Finally, there is the still further point that the *Shin Byu* ceremony is the act not only of an individual, and of a social community, but also of a religious order. In this ritual, the role of the child – Everyman's and Everywoman's son – symbolizes that each one of us is involved, at first hand, in this drama of living on earth, participant on the one hand in its tumults and its vicissitudes and exactions and its routines, its transience and decay, but participant also in an enduring quality that transcends the mundane, and lifts us, or can lift us, out of the utterly mundane and contingent; and that this quality is moral. It reminds us that in righteous living, human beings have a window on eternity.

This point applies to everyone individually, and must be re-enacted over and over again as each new generation, each new person, comes along. It applies also to the whole society, so that the community participates again and again in each one of its members' personal involvement.

Nonetheless, it is not only the person, and not only the group, whose involvement constitutes the ceremony. They are accepting it, and repeating it; but they are not creating it. They are involved, but it is oriented not to them, but to the Buddha. In the identification with him they are affirming that their recognition of the moral law is not their own whim, and is not just their society's tradition; rather it is given to them, by someone who, they affirm, not only, like them, set out in this direction, but, unlike them, arrived at the goal. There is a subtlety here, and I am not confident that I can make my meaning clear. The faith of Buddhists is involved and there has been virtually nothing in our Western tradition to help us to see the validity or even the significance of a religious faith that we do not personally share. Yet let me try: I personally see a profound significance in the fact that these Buddhists are identifying themselves with a man who, if only in their own assertion, not only went out in search of Truth, but found it, so that their assurance of the validity of "going out" rests not merely on their sense of adumbrations of eternity, but on an equal and final assurance that the going does in fact lead somewhere; and indeed, somewhere supremely good.

People without faith, or without firm faith, sometimes speak of religious traditions in terms of human beings' search. This is not adequate for traditions such as the Christian or Jewish or Islamic traditions, which rest on a concept of revelation; but neither is it quite adequate here. Although these Buddhists do not talk of revelation and do not even talk of God, they keep their tradition alive by bringing to it afresh each generation, for now two thousand five hundred years, a live conviction that their quest is not merely a quest, but is guaranteed, as it were, by the Buddha's Buddhahood.

I wonder whether you see the importance that I do in the living assurance here that someone has shown the way, having traveled it. Thereby this has become not a guess, but a discovery; not a groping, but a joyous affirmation.

Now, this remains true, and you and I can recognize it as such, quite apart from any question of whether or not we are Buddhists. Our capacity to see its significance and even its validity does not turn on our accepting any doctrine about the Buddha. One might almost be tempted to say that this aspect of the ceremony is made true not by what the Buddha accomplished, but by the faith of followers in his having accomplished it. Certainly their faith today in what transcends themselves is crucial, and is creative. We need not agree with them on any metaphysical role that the Buddha played in the long-ago past, in what to many of us has been a remote corner of the world; and yet we may recognize the metaphysical role that he is playing today in human lives. And we may recognize the significance of their faith – and in this faith even an outsider may share – that such a role is ideally there, to be filled. What I am suggesting is that there is a metaphysical truth in the faith of these Buddhists, which is independent of the historical truths of their belief.

I close, then, hoping that perhaps this brief presentation may have helped readers to feel that once we have learned the form, we ourselves could reasonably participate, at least imaginatively, in such a ceremony as the *Shin Byu*, or at least could empathize with those who do; that here, something within each of us is significantly touched, so that this ritual of a distant group makes sense.

And may I add that the more genuine and more live our own personal religious faith – of whatever form – the more sense it makes; and the more sense being a Buddhist makes.

Muslims

Almost any visitor to India interested in the religious life of its people will note a striking difference architecturally between a Hindu temple and a Muslim mosque. The temple is apt to be ornate, even florid. Its involute complexity suggests that truth is much more elaborate than one had supposed, and it denies nothing, not even incongruity. Very different is the stark simplicity of the Muslim place of worship. The mighty Imperial Mosque in Delhi, for example, is a structure whose artistic impressiveness and power come from the use of straight lines and simple curves, splendidly graceful and yet austerely disciplined. Certainly it is brilliantly conceived and its impact is immediate: one grasps at once the balance and dignity, the spacious reverence, the serenity of its straightforward affirmation. Its architect's vision of the glory of God, and of humanity's service due to Him,[14] is evidently an ordered vision.

Such a point is confirmed if one has the privilege of witnessing a service in such a mosque, especially at one of the great festival prayers, where perhaps a hundred thousand people array themselves in neat lines and bow in precise unison as token of their personal and corporate submission to the will of God, which is definite and sure.

A similar contrast can be seen in the realm of doctrine. For a Hindu, there are various systems of ideas, involute, elaborate, and regarded as always tentative, from among which one may choose. In contrast, the Muslim community symbolizes its belief in probably the simplest, tidiest, "creed" in all the world. I am sure that most readers will have heard it: "There is no god but God, and Muhammad is God's apostle." The Muslims themselves refer to this two-clause affirmation simply as "the two words," or even "the word." And while this may be carrying compression just a trifle far, still it is certainly as succinct and clean as one could hope to find.

Because of its centrality, and its neatness, this simple "creed" may well provide us with the item for our consideration here of the Muslims. As with other religious communities, so with the Islamic community, we choose one element from the formal pattern of their faith, in the hope that, exploring it, we may find that it can lead us, if not to the heart of their religious life, at least into its precincts, and can suggest something of the richness of what lies behind. What better emblem of the Muslim's faith, for our purposes, than this crystallized "creed," which the Muslims themselves have chosen to sum up their vision? To repeat this "creed" is, formally, to become a Muslim; perhaps to understand it is to understand a Muslim. Or let me put the point more realistically: to begin to understand it may be to go some distance, at least, towards understanding the position of those whose faith it typifies.

In suggesting the coherence and simplicity of the Muslim confession of faith, I do not wish to suggest that it is limited or lacks profundity. A mosque may be very intricately decorated – fine interlacing arabesques and the endlessly delicate complexities of an elaborate calligraphy usually embroider the arches and the walls – yet these decorations, however ornate in themselves, are regularly held in strict subordination to an overall pattern that is essentially simple, so that detail is organized into a coherent unity. This is similarly the case in the realm of philosophers and theologians constructing elaborate systems of ideas. The names of Avicenna and Averroes are probably the best known in the West, but there are also many others who worked out in careful detail impressive structures of thought. There were also meticulously elaborate systems of law, comprehensive and ramified. But again, these were subordinate to the higher truth, the simpler truth, of the "creed." As one gets closer to truth, one gets closer to God; and God is one. He is majestic, mighty, awesome, merciful, and much more, but above all, for the Muslim, He is one. Every other sin, the theologians affirm, may be forgiven us, but not that of *shirk*, which is not merely "polytheism" as it is often translated but the worship of false so-called gods instead of God, the failure to recognize that the final truth and power of the universe is one.

Before we turn to questions of meaning, which are of course our chief concern, let us note a few points about the formula as a formula. I suppose that every effective religious symbol is not only inexhaustibly meaningful in what it stands for, but is also in some ways intrinsically interesting in itself. This one certainly is. We have already remarked that it is short. It is also pungent and crisp. In the original Arabic (the language in which it is always used, no matter what the actual language of the people concerned, from Indonesian to African Swahili, from South Indian Malayalam to Turkish) it is resonant and rolling, packing quite a punch. It so happens that of the fifteen syllables, about half begin with an "l" sound, or end with it, or both. This liquid alliteration, added to the rhyme and to a very marked rhythm, is forceful. *La-'i-lá-ha-'il-lal-láh; Mu-ham-ma-dur-ra-sú-lul-láh.*

Then there is a calligraphic point. In the Arabic alphabet, which is anyway highly decorative, it so happens that this particular set of words when written out is strikingly patterned, and lends itself to picturesque presentation.

The creedal formula is certainly in constant service. For example, it is whispered in the ears of the newborn baby, so that its affirmation may be the first words that a Muslim shall hear on entering this world. And between then and its use at his or her funeral, that person, alone and in community, will hear it, and pronounce it, often and often and often. And apart from its ceremonial and, as it were, sacred use, it can be found in everyday affairs also. I remember a scene in India some years ago when one summer my wife and I were at a mountain resort in the Himalayas, and were out for a hike in the hills; we came upon a work-gang busy in the construction of a rude mountain road. It was, of course, all hand labor; they had crushed the stones with hammers, and were now rolling them with a large heavy roller. Rather in the fashion of sailors working to a sea shanty, they were rhythmically pulling this heavy roller in spurts of concerted effort: the foreman would sing out *La ilaha illa 'llah*, and the rest of the gang, then, would put their shoulders to the ropes and with a heave would respond *Muhammadur rasulu 'llah*. This went on and on, as they continued to work with a will and with good strong heaves. *La ilaha illa 'llah* he would chant; *Muhammadur rasulu 'llah* would come the vigorous response. Such a scene represents, of course, a kind of living in which a split into religious and secular has not come to segment life. At a different level are the formal ceremonies in the weekly service of some of the Islamic Sufi orders, in which the initiate devotees will induce a mystic ecstasy or trance by a solemn and rhythmic repetition or incantation of the formula.

Between these two comes a religious use such as that by the *mu'azzin* in his call five times a day to prayer. Its sonorous recitative from the minaret punctuates village or town life and summons the faithful to turn for a moment from their routine affairs to the life of the spirit.

I have called this "creed" a symbol; and in some ways it plays in Muslim life a role similar to that played, for instance, for Christians by the cross. Nonetheless it is not a pictorial sign but a verbal one, and this itself is significant and appropriate. The role of linguistic form, of words, in Islamic religious life is quite special. I have already spoken of the written word – calligraphy – as a typical Muslim art form. This community has carried the decorative use of writing probably further than has any other people. And take revelation itself: in the Christian case this takes the form of a person, whereas for the Muslim it too is verbal. In the Qur'an, God makes Himself and His purpose known to humankind in the form of words (highly meaningful words, of course; one could equally say, in the form of ideas). It is altogether appropriate, then, that the chief symbol of Islam should also be verbal.

So far, I have allowed myself to follow the usual Western practice of calling this two-phrase synopsis of the Muslim's faith a "creed." To do this is not altogether misleading, though you will have seen that its place in Muslim life is only very partly correlative with that of the "creed" for Christians. It is time now, however, to modify this still further. We all need to see more carefully ways in which the faith of other people is expressed in patterns that do not quite correspond to our own – or to what we expect of them.

In some ways, then, the "two words" of the Islamic assertion do constitute a "creed," a statement of belief, but in other ways they do not; and the Muslims do not themselves call this formula a "creed." They call it, rather, a "witness." Regularly the statement is preceded by the words "I bear witness that there is no god but" and so on. And even when this actual clause is not employed, when nothing is added, an idea of witnessing is involved, and can be quite basic. The Islamic community has been one of the five great missionary communities in human history (along with the Buddhist and the Christian, and in recent times the Marxist and the secular communities); and the idea of bearing witness to one's faith is quite central to a Muslim's attitudes. His or her assertion is not so much an affirmation of belief, as a proclamation – of conviction. And in a subtle fashion, there is involved here a point that, I have come to recognize, is more basic in all religious life than is usually realized. It is this: that it is not so much that the Muslim believes that God is one, and Muhammad is His prophet, as it is that he or she takes this for granted. They presuppose it, and go on from there. From their own point of view, one might almost say that, so far as they are concerned, they know that these things are so, and what they are doing is simply announcing them, bearing witness to them; and affirming that their lives are, will be, ordered in terms of them.

The same kind of thing is true, it turns out, of all religious life. One distorts a Christian's faith, for example, by saying simply that he or she believes Jesus Christ to be divine, to be the son of God. Those concerned have over the centuries said rather that they recognize this – that these are the facts, and they have been fortunate enough to see them. In the Christian case the matter has become complicated by the fact that in most Western languages the verb *credo*, "I believe," and so on, has come, since the eighteenth century or so, to be used both for intellectual belief and for religious faith – though persons of faith have tried to insist that "belief that" and "belief in" are two different matters. Certainly true faith has already begun to crumble somewhat, if it has not actually gone, as soon as people have reduced what used to be the data, the presuppositions, of their worldview to a set of true-or-false propositions: when what was once the presupposed context for a transcending religious faith becomes rather the foreground of intellectual belief (true or false). This is one of the fundamental troubles in the modern world, and a fundamental problem arising from a recognition of religious diversity – that what used to be unconscious premises become, rather, scrutinized intellectualizations. At this new level, believers begin to wonder if they really "believe," in this new sense (and often enough find that actually they do not).[15]

In the Islamic case, as in the Jewish, the word of God is, fundamentally, an imperative. Even the proclamation of God's oneness is in some ways more a command, to worship (in their vocabulary) Him alone, than merely an invitation to believe that He is there alone. Faith differs from belief in many ways, and goes beyond it; one way is that faith in God's oneness is a recognition of His unique and exclusive authority, and an active giving of oneself to it. Like the Christian, the classical Muslim theologian has seen faith as a commitment. He would understand at once St. James in the New Testament writing, "You believe that God is one? You do well: the devils also recognize ['believe' here is a mistranslation[16]] and tremble."[17] To a truly religious person, the question is not one merely of seeing the facts – let alone merely of believing this or that – but of doing something about it.

Having said that, however, we on the outside may still ask what others' presuppositions are: what is presumed by those within the community, as they go on to recognition and commitment.

We find ourselves having come round, then, to the question that we earlier postponed, the question of the meaning of the "two words." What does it mean to say "There is no god but God, and Muhammad is His apostle"? What does it mean, that is, to a Muslim – to someone to whom these two clauses are not merely true, but profoundly and cosmically true, are the two most important and final truths in the world, and the most crucial for human beings and their destiny? Let us look at each in turn.

To say that there is one God, and that He alone is to be worshiped, means at its most immediate, as it meant in pagan Arabia when it was first proclaimed, a rejection of polytheism and idolatry. When Muhammad captured Mecca in 630 C.E., and set up Islam in triumph, he gave a general amnesty to the human beings there who had resisted his cause and were now defeated, but he smashed without quarter the idols in the shrine of the Ka'bah – three hundred and sixty, it is said, figures of the pagans' gods. From that day to this, Islam has been uncompromising in its doctrine of monotheism, and its insistence on transcendence: God the Creator and Judge is Lord of all the universe, is high above all His creatures and beyond them, and beyond all their imaginings – and certainly beyond all their representations. Other deities, it asserts, are but the figments of human beings' wayward imagination, are unadulterated fiction; they just do not exist. One must not bow down to them or worship them, or look to them for help. God is God alone; on this point Islam is positive, emphatic, and clear.

Historically, as the Islamic movement has spread, across the centuries, from Arabia through the Near East and into Central Asia and has penetrated China, into India and South-East Asia, across Africa and still today is spreading, down into Africa and elsewhere, it has met polytheism in many forms, has attacked it and replaced it. Like the Church in the Roman Empire and Northern Europe, and later in the Americas, so Islam in large parts of the world has superseded polytheistic practice and thought with monotheistic.

At a subtler level, for those capable of seeing it, the doctrine has meant also at times, and certainly ought to mean, a rejection of human tyranny. God alone is to be worshiped, to be served. For the person for whom this faith is sufficiently vivid, this can mean that no earthly power, no human figure, deserves or can legitimately claim one's allegiance; and any attempt to impose a purely human yoke on a community's necks is an infringement not only of human dignity but of cosmic order, and to submit to it would be sin. Admittedly there has been, especially in periods of decline, an alternative interpretation whereby God's governance of affairs is taken as determining not what ought to be but what is. This view has led to fatalism – a passive acceptance of whatever happens. Perhaps readers will feel that I am intruding my own predilections here in siding with those Muslims who have taken rather the activist line, asserting God's will as something to be striven for, as was done more widely in Islam's earlier centuries, and is beginning to be done again in our own day. You will agree, in any case, that it is legitimate and proper, in interpreting others' faith as in one's own, to try to see it at its best and highest. That at least is what I am trying to do throughout these essays.

There is still a third level of meaning, which was stressed particularly by the Sufi mystics in the medieval period, and is beginning to get wide support today. According to this view, to worship God alone is to turn aside from false gods not only in the concrete sense of idols and religious polytheism, but also in the subtler sense of turning aside as well from a moral polytheism, from false values – the false gods of the heart. To pursue merely earthly goals, to value them, to give them one's allegiance and in a sense to worship them – goals such as wealth, prestige, sex, national aggrandizement, comfort, or all the other distractions and foibles of human life – this, says the sensitive Muslim conscience, like the sensitive Christian or Jewish one, is to infringe the principle of monotheism. Similarly, to look for help to purely mundane forces, to rely upon armies or devious stratagems, to trust anything that is not intrinsically good – this is to have more than one god. The affirmation that God alone is to be worshiped means, for the person of true piety and rigorous sincerity, that no other objective must claim one's effort or loyalty; one must fear no other power, honor no other prize, pursue no other goal.

I would mention, finally, one other interpretation of the "no god but God" phrase, one that again has been put forward by some of the mystics. This one has not been widespread, even among these; yet I mention it because I personally find it attractive, and it shows the kind of thing that can be done. This particular view is in line with the general position taken by the mystics that the religious life is a process, a movement in faith. According to this interpretation, then, the statement that "there is no god but God" is to be taken in stages. No one, this reading suggests, can legitimately and truly say "God" who has not previously said, and meant, "no god." To arrive at true faith, one must first pass through a stage of unbelief. "There is no god:" this comes first, and must be lived through in all sincerity, and all terror. A person brought up in a religious tradition must have seen through that tradition, its forms and fancies, its shams and shibboleths; must have learned the bleakness of atheism, and have experienced its meaninglessness and eventually its dread. Only such a person is able to go on, perhaps only years later, to a faith that is without superficiality and without glibness, is not merely cheap and second-hand. If one has said "there is no god" with the anguish of a genuine despair, one may then, with God's grace, go on to say "but God," and say it with the ecstasy of genuine insight.

"No god" here may well be taken not necessarily in the theist sense of God, but as that above or within or underlying us in which we recognize that we have cause to have faith – as in the aphorism "the only true atheist is one who loves no one and whom no one loves, who cares for no truth, sees no beauty, strives for no justice, knows no courage and no joy, finds no meaning, and has lost all hope."

Let us turn, next, to the second proposition: "Muhammad is the apostle of God." The first thing to grasp here is that this is a statement not about Muhammad's status but about his function. The Islamic concept of "apostle," or "prophet," is quite special; and one is misled if one too readily assumes that this corresponds to ideas familiar already in the West. The underlying notion here, and it is tacitly presupposed by the formulation, is that God has something to say to humankind, and has from time to time chosen certain persons in various communities through whom to say it. The assertion here is that Muhammad was one of those persons. It too, then, is in significant degree, and even primarily, a statement about God. As the theologians worked it out, it involves the conviction – recognition, from their point of view – that God is not essentially passive, inscrutable, content to remain transcendent; rather, that from all eternity, and as part of His very nature, He is the kind of God who has something to say to humankind. What He has to say is what Westerners would call the moral law. When He created the universe and when He created humanity, He did not exactly create the moral law, for this comes closer to being, rather, a part of Himself – but anyway He ordained it, or set it forth.

This is the prime affirmation. Along with it, He created human beings to receive the moral awareness, free and responsible to carry it out. He communicated this moral law to humankind. He did not leave us to grope about in the dark, to discover for ourselves, by our own efforts, what we could. No; God Himself acted, and spoke – spoke through the mouths of the prophets and apostles, beginning with Adam; that is, from the very beginning of history. As remarked in our first chapter, religion is nowadays sometimes spoken of as the human search for God. On this, the Islamic position is like the Jewish and the Christian positions, rejecting such a view emphatically, and asserting rather that God takes the initiative. As Micah put it, in the Judaeo-Christian tradition, "He hath shown thee, O man, what is good." Humanity's business in the religious life is not a quest but a response.

Thirdly, in the message that God communicated is to be found, in the Muslim view, not what is true so much, though of course they do hold this, but what is right. The position differs from the Christian one in that it is a revelation *from* God, more than *of* God. The apostle or prophet is one who conveys to humankind the message that God wants us to know; namely, how we should live. Accordingly, out of the message theoreticians and systematizers eventually extracted and constructed a law, finally (after several centuries) elaborated in all detail and ultimately (especially in recent times) turned into a static system.

One last point, and with this I close. I wrote a moment ago that the phrase "Muhammad is the apostle of God" is a statement not about Muhammad's status so much as about his function. Let me elaborate this just a little. The position stands over against the quite different Christian orientation, which sees the person of Christ as central and ultimate, pre-existent and divine. Muslims also posit a central and ultimate truth, pre-existent and divine, namely the Qur'an – not a person but a book, or better, what the book says. Muhammad plays in the Islamic scheme the role played in the Christian system by St. Paul or St. Peter; namely, that of an apostle who proclaims on earth God's gift to humankind, which in the Islamic case is the scripture. In contrast to the Christian conviction, one might almost say that the Muslims' affirmation about their prophet is not a statement about Muhammad's person at all, but about the Qur'an; about "what Muhammad brought." To say that he is an apostle, sent by God, is to affirm these things that we have noted about God, and about the kind of universe that we live in, and about the human situation, and morality; and then within that framework it is to assert further that the message purveyed by Muhammad is authentic. If you hold this, then you are accepting as incumbent upon you in an ultimate moral sense the practical duties that flow from this tradition. For you are recognizing the obligation to perform them as not of human but of divine origin. Those of us for whom the content of morality is not defined in this historical source should nonetheless not allow this to obscure from us the cosmic things that those inspired from this source are saying about morality, about what it means to be human, and about God.

The Chinese

In these inquiries into the religious life of the world, we have in each case been singling out one symbol of a community's stance, and exploring it – hoping that it might serve as a rewarding clue to the religious orientation of that group. For China I have chosen the ancient *yin-yang* circle.

Unlike the symbols that we have considered in our other presentations, this is not a ceremony nor a phrase, but a pictorial design, a visual image. In some ways this facilitates our task, since we in the West are quite accustomed to the use of visual images in religious symbolism, and indeed think of this as altogether standard and appropriate. Moreover, we see perhaps more clearly with visual images than in the case of any other type of religious symbol that the item is indeed symbolic – a representation pointing beyond itself, and capable of meaning different things to different people, depending on their upbringing and on their capacity and insight, and the quality of their personal life. We know that an image means more to a believer than to an outsider; much more to a profound and devout believer than the same image does or can mean to a lukewarm or superficial one; and indeed, that the meaning lies not in the image itself but in what the person of faith brings to it and carries away from it. We are not quite so trained to recognize that this sort of thing is true also of a theological system, for instance; though such a system, too, I personally take as symbolic, this time an intellectual symbol (the Greek word for a Christian "creed" is *symbolon*). One does well to see it as something whose meaning lies beyond the immediate sense of its statements: the phrases in themselves mean something, but symbolize something more – as in poetry.

On the other hand, we are at a certain disadvantage in considering a visual image, since I am simply writing about it, while of course such an image is meant not to be written about but to be looked at. It would be much more effective if all of us could have the actual *yin-yang* circle not only in front of our eyes throughout our discussion, but indeed had grown up with it, in the presence of family and friends and community to whom its symbolic richness was massive. Not only is it extremely simple, like any good religious symbol, whereas my verbal comments upon its meaning may become complex and elaborate. Furthermore, it is graceful, and serenely quiet. This, indeed, is part of its point; and I am afraid that my endeavors to interpret it, even if they succeed in catching something of the import, will yet lack, certainly, the simplicity and the charm.

I imagine that most people have seen the image. Take a circle, and divide it in two equal and congruent parts by drawing an S-shaped curve from top to bottom, so that you have two as it were curved tear-drops nestling one against the other. One should be black and the other white; or, if you have color, one red and the other black. You may if you like put a dot of white in the middle of the largest bulbous part of the black, and a black dot in the white, suggesting that each half of the circle lightly touches or invades the other. You are left with a perfectly symmetrical figure, such that you cannot say whether it is a black circle with a graceful white tear-drop in it, or a white circle with a graceful black tear-drop; or two contrasting tear-drops so interposed as to constitute together a perfect whole, flaw-lessly circular, or a perfect circle divided into two equal, contrasting, interpenetrating, and lovely parts.

With its total balance, and its endless, sinuous curves, it is a superb synthesis of rest and movement, of contrast and concord, of immediacy and ultimacy.

Before we go on to probe the symbolism, may I comment on a prior point? It is a Western convention to talk of the religions of the world, imagining these as so many distinct entities, each a system of its own. Within such a framework, Westerners have learned to speak of three religions in China, and to label these Confucianist, Taoist, and Buddhist. Once this pattern has been set up, it is then broken down again when one says that a Chinese person may belong to all three at once, which leaves one just a trifle perplexed. As you see, I am not fol-lowing this custom. I have deliberately entitled this essay "The Chinese," rather than using any one of the specific names of religious traditions there. Further, in order to represent the religious life of that people as typically and as faithfully as any one item could, I have chosen a sym-bol that is not specifically Confucian, or Taoist, or Buddhist. It has been used by all three groups, more copi-ously in Taoist lore perhaps than in the teaching or prac-tice of the other two traditions, but certainly not exclu-sively; and actually it is considerably more ancient in China than any of these. Its use can be traced far back into the dim past, before the rise or introduction of any one of the three great traditions, though it is now part of them all. By choosing it, then, we illustrate the pervasive catholicity of the religious orientation of the Chinese. Indeed, as we shall see presently, the symbol itself repre-sents and affirms the harmonious holding together of contrasts in a balanced synthesis, the integrating of divergence into a rounded whole.

But this is to anticipate. Originally, and most immediately, the image represents *yang* and *yin*, the two fundamental principles in Chinese cosmology. *Yang* is hot, dry, active, light, and masculine; *yin* is cold, moist, passive, dark, and feminine. *Yang* is movement; *yin* is rest. The interplay of these two principles produces the five elements of fire, metal, earth, wood, and water; and these in turn in varying proportions combine to produce everything that is. Fire is almost pure *yang*, water is almost pure *yin* – almost, but not quite; for nothing exists that does not combine something of both. I have called them principles, but they have also been termed modes. And not only every substance, but also every event, is a combination of the two. Heaven is more *yang*, earth more *yin*. Man is more *yang*, woman more *yin*. Victory is more *yang*, peace more *yin*. They may also be regarded as phases, ever succeeding one another in endless revolution and in infinite variety. Night and day, summer and winter, male and female, stability and change – the universe as a whole and in all its parts, its being and its becoming, all is an expression of the underlying *yin* and *yang* in eternal interplay. There is nothing in which *yin* and *yang* do not participate.

Now this theory of *yang-yin* has been widely used in all sorts of contexts in China: as a hocus-pocus in elaborate superstitions, as a basic notion in systematic scientific thought, as an intellectual framework for brilliant and profound philosophy. It would be out of place for us here to follow up the superstition side, in line with my general policy of trying to consider religious life at its most spiritual, not at its most ordinary or debased. So far as science is concerned, of course early Chinese awareness in this realm, though historically of major world consequence, has long since been superseded; but it is perhaps worth mentioning that some observers hold that twentieth-century science in the West is moving closer to a fundamental *yin-yang* type of interpretation of the natural universe than traditional Western views – we shall presently be returning to this, briefly.

So far as Chinese philosophy goes, I shall do no more than mention the name of Chu Hsi, the twelfth-century thinker at the time of the Sung Renascence who reformulated the classical tradition of learning in China into what is now called Neo-Confucianism. His powerful and lucid system of thought lasted until our own day as the chief formulation of China's more or less national ideology. He constructed it on a basis of which the *yin-yang* idea was a part.

But our concern is with the *yang-yin* circle as a religious symbol. And as with symbols in other traditions that we have considered, I shall not try to exhaust or even to systematize all the things that it can mean or has meant to diverse groups that have cherished it. Rather I shall simply explore some avenues that it opens up, so as to get some insight into the faith and some sympathy with the attitude of persons whose outlook has been different from that traditional in the West. Indeed, we shall concentrate on only one significance, since I find this basic and deeply illuminating. It is the notion of what I call complement dualism.

We in the West are familiar with another type of dualism, which we may call conflict dualism. In this, two basic forces are in collision, as opposites that struggle and clash: good and evil, right and wrong, black and white, true and false. This type of dualism seems to have its origin about the middle of the first millennium B.C.E. in the Tigris–Euphrates valley or in Iran. There the traditions from Zarathustra (or "Zoroaster") formulated it into a metaphysics, a dichotomy which split the cosmos into two opposing forces led respectively by Ahura Mazda and Angra Mainyu – or God and the Devil. In other forms, sometimes considerably modified, it found its way into the Jewish, Christian, and Islamic traditions, and has been vigorously resuscitated in recent times on a world scale by Marxism. In the religious traditions a Devil, over against God, was long accepted; Heaven and Hell are postulated, as well as the saved and the damned, the sheep and the goats. In the Marxist case there is a variation on this kind of outlook; Marxism rejects metaphysics, and yet interprets this world in terms of dualist conflict: the class struggle, *bourgeoisie* and proletariat, capitalism and communism, exploiters and exploited, thesis and antithesis. In the religious and in the Marxist versions, a final unity, whether synthesis or ultimate triumph of one side, is envisaged; but meanwhile the world is analyzed in bipolar terms. For two and a half thousand years the Near East and the Western worlds have either postulated or sympathized with a cosmic conflict dualism; or, in a dichotomy of less antagonism, with a dualism of opposition. If not God and the Devil, at least God and the world, matter and spirit, either/or, the human and nature (in traditional English, "man and nature;" nowadays we would be inclined to say "the human and the rest of nature").

India has never quite understood this, and its basic orientation has been monistic. For Indians, reality is not two, but ultimately one, and meanwhile pluralist. Even religious assertions are thought of not as true or false, but as more or less approximate: the world is not black and white, but a panorama, not of grey but of reds and greens and yellows. The difference is much more radical and more pervasive than the West usually allows, between India on this matter and the West with its yes-or-no approach to life. The *yin-yang* circle of China which we are at present considering symbolizes another view. It is dualist, but the dualism is of a different type; one that is, I think, radically different from both India and the West, and is worth our trying to understand.

Let us look at that circle once again. The light and the dark are distinct, are in contrast; but not in conflict. They combine to form a rounded whole. The form of each presupposes the other. The direction of each is towards the area of the other, but as it moves both move, in a rhythmic cycle of phased and balanced symmetry.

Let us take as one example the question of the human and nature. If you do not see what I mean by looking at this *yang-yin* image of the circle, look instead at any typical Chinese painting, perhaps of a quiet fisherman by a waterfall where with subtle restrained suggestion and in a few incredibly delicate touches the person merges into the landscape, and the beauty lies in a sense of utter peace found in a union of person with nature. In the Western tradition there are, of course, exceptions; but certainly one of the dominant motifs has been, in contrast, that of the human against nature – out of which has grown our ruthlessly applied technology. We regard nature if not as something against which to struggle, at least as something to subordinate and to control, and to use. (Not merely technology: science itself has been characterized as experimenting with things in order to control; or at least as a pitting of one's wits against the world around us.) On the religious side of the Western heritage, the outlook is expressed in the first chapter of Genesis, where God is pictured as creating man and woman and setting them on earth and saying, "Be fruitful and multiply, and fill the earth and subdue it; and have dominion." The *yin-yang* circle symbolizes a different mood.

Similarly, in the West the concept God is of course one of ultimate importance; whereas in China this kind of concept has not been particularly significant or much developed. This does not mean that the Chinese have been less religious than the West; rather that they have been religious in a different way, and have conceptualized their faith in a different way. With us, God creates the world, out of nothing. It stands over against man and woman; and even these, though created in God's image, remain creatures, with God sometimes conceived as the "Wholly Other." In the *yang-yin* circle before us you might say that there is nothing to correspond to the Western concept "God;" or alternatively, you might say that in so far as this concept signifies perfection, what corresponds is the circle itself, the whole, the symmetry and balance, the perfection of the various parts.

Again, if we take the concept Tao, which is in a sense ultimate reality or ultimate value for many Chinese (and not only Taoists), one thing to say about it is that it signifies the way (*tao* means "way") in which the *yin-yang* process operates. It has been remarked that the Chinese have felt that the universe is quite capable of looking after itself, of functioning on its own. In so far as this signifies that it does not need a power or person outside itself to run it, the point is valid. But the way in which the functioning dependably and beautifully proceeds is profoundly significant for the Chinese, is a final truth. It is, if you like, for them an object of faith. The *yang-yin* circle at which we are looking is after all a circle – not a jagged or chaotic mess, as the modern atheist without faith is beginning to suspect that the world is. To represent totality as an harmonious perfection in movement is no mean affirmation.

Or let us take the question of good or evil. It has been not unknown in China that *yang* in this dualism has represented or been associated with good, or the good spirits, and *yin* with evil, or the demons. More basic and more representative, however, has been the view that in this symbol good is represented by the harmony of the contrasting parts. Evil would be an absence of that harmony. In this sense, and it is the dominant one, the symbol is what we might call idealist, representing the universe as it ought to be; the actual state of human affairs, things as they are, would then be represented presumably by such a circle in which the S-curve is out of proportion, or all askew or jagged. Human morality – of which you may be sure the Chinese, and not least the Taoists, have not been unaware! – is that which introduces distortion into the natural harmony of the world. The two halves of our symbol, then, are not good and evil; both are good, and a further good lies in their due proportion. Evil is not the opposite of good, it is the absence or dislocation of good.

Our image, then, symbolizes, for instance, male and female; and to one who has meditated upon it and seen truth through it, it is meaningless to ask whether man is better than woman, or vice versa, and it is wrong to think in terms of a conflict between them. Both are necessary; each is defined in terms of the other; each is fulfilled in a totality that both constitute. And evil in this realm occurs if the integrity of either part, or the integrity of the two

together, is infringed. Similar considerations apply to problems of the individual and society; of stability and change;
abiding truth and ceaseless flux.

In area after area of life, both moral and intellectual,
this image symbolizes a faith in a dualism of complement
rather than of conflict.

By faith I mean in part a way of looking at the world.
A few pages back we spoke of this on the intellectual side
in science, and remarked that there seemed perhaps some
justification for thinking, as some have suggested, that the
yin-yang symbol serves to represent an intellectual outlook
that makes increasing sense in the scientific field. I do not
know enough science to speak here more than very tenta-
tively, but it does seem that in several areas scientists have
been moving away from a sharp opposition-dichotomy outlook towards one rather of the complementarity of opposites. I suppose the most obvious example is the positive
and negative electric charge, each of which is defined in
terms of the other, and of which the *yang-yin* symbol would
be perhaps a fairly reasonable presentation. Another
instance might be the wave theory and the quantum theory
of light, each of which is valid though partial, while a uni-
fied view embraces both. Even the distinction between true
and false is not nearly so sharp in science as it used to be in
our pre-scientific tradition: scientific measurements, for
instance, are regarded, rather, as correct to a certain degree
of accuracy.

Other subtler dichotomies that have been losing their
sharpness are those between organism and environment,
which we now see as together constituting a reality; or in
philosophy, take traditional issues such as freedom and
determinism. This problem used to be put in such a way as
to presume that an intelligent person must choose: either

this or that. Nowadays one has to hold the two notions, if they are valid at all, in some different sort of mutual relation, not as clear-cut alternatives; freedom and determinism together in constant interplay constitute our life. Similarly in psychosomatic medicine and psychology: mind and body (our traditional terms) are seen as referring not to two distinct entities opposed to each other, or even separate, but as two interacting components dynamically constituting a total circle. Again, a century ago science and religion themselves were set up so as to seem to many people to be alternatives in bitter conflict; whereas today many feel that a truer view would see them (or at least, see the scientific and the spiritual) as two different but complementary elements revolving in a larger, and dynamic, whole. It is an interesting affirmation, symbolically imaged, that, of the universe as a whole or any part of it, there are always two seemingly contrasting facets or modes of which neither is complete without the other, and of which both taken together in due balance constitute the truth.

However this may be, the more interesting and immediately relevant aspects of the matter for our purposes are the moral ones; and among these, not least significant are the political. I think that we must not underestimate the significance of the outlook that is here involved, even for practical and immediate affairs. There are many, many people who have no idea that their actions are influenced by metaphysical traditions which they certainly could not themselves state, and in which they probably do not suppose themselves to be interested; and yet such people often react to events and behave on most major issues in ways that in fact are related to inherited presuppositions such as those here at stake. In the Cold War phase of twentieth-century history, foreign policy was regularly based on a

presupposition of conflict dualism. Such policy was widely accepted, many having been brought up to see the
world in terms of black and white in conflict or opposition. I personally would be much happier if I felt that the
world's major political leaders were sitting down to pon-
der global problems or issues in which they or their
nations or tribes are implicated having spent half an hour
or more contemplating with some sort of religious faith
the *yin-yang* circle of balanced contrast; or (having been
brought up on such a symbol since childhood) took it for
granted that ultimate truth lies in harmony. And certainly
it is a significant matter that China has passed into the
hands of rulers who, being Marxist, would reject this
internal tradition in favor of an Armageddon-type ideology that is either/or, and that reads history, and plans policy in terms of clash and struggle. For them life is not coexistence but conflict.

I should like to close this chapter with reference to the
point at which we began, that of religious diversity. The
Chinese have not been unaware of contrasts between the
teachings of, let us say, K'ung Fu-tse and Lao-tse, from
whom the Confucianist and Taoist traditions respectively
stem. As our circle symbolizes, however, they usually comprehend both these within the compass of a larger whole.
And when Buddhist teaching arrived from India, and many
were won to it, they added it as a third component in the
amalgam. In the modern world it is possible to argue that
all humankind must learn to see religious diversity in this
way (and secularists, in a way that adopts the perceived sec-
ularity–religion polarity), so that we may construct on earth
an encircling concord and fellowship that recognizes differences, and even contrasts, in the religious (or the secu-
lar/religious) realm as parts within an harmonious circle of

worldwide human community and within a transcending
circle of truth – the truth lying not with one element in the
complex but in the adjustment of each to the others. This
is a question that we must face in our next chapter.

In the meantime I may remark that of course this
view is opposed by those who see such a solution as a
betrayal of one's own loyalties. They assert that truth is
truth, and must be upheld, it must not be dissolved in
camaraderie. The debate between these two could become
quite sharp: between the universalist and the particularist.
As I have said, we shall be returning to this problem in
another connection.

For the moment, however, let me relate it to our present concern, our Chinese symbol. What I myself see in
the *yang-yin* symbol with regard to this matter, if I may
be allowed this personal note, is not the first solution
only, not merely an image that would reduce Christian
truth, for instance, to a part of some larger whole.
Rather, I find it a circle embracing, for Christian truth
itself, and for the others, both this liberal universalism
and at the same time the exclusivist interpretation – the
two in constant interplay. Its point is to deny that one has
to choose between orthodoxy and liberalism, between
loyalty to one's own vision of faith in its particularity,
and loyalty to others' vision in its variety. An effete and
watered-down eclecticism that is substituted for Christian
or Jewish or secular or any other orthodoxy is no final
solution. A truly Christian attitude to outsiders must
involve both the validity of Christian orthodoxy (shorn
of its exclusivism) and an acceptance of persons of other
orthodoxies as one's siblings, and their vision, like one's
own, as valid though not complete – in one's own eyes,
and in the eyes of God. In this, the image says to me that,

as in all ultimate matters, truth lies not in an either/or, but in a both/and.

Implications for Oneself and
One's Own Community

In considering the faith of others, there comes a point when one may ask, as I propose to ask now, how all this impinges on one's own faith – or lack of it. One's own development is at stake in all learning; and learning about others' views of the world may well modify, a little or a great deal, one's own view of it. In each of the previous chapters I have taken one item to illustrate the whole. Here, my suggestion is that we illustrate our involvement in this issue of pluralism by considering one instance of the general situation. Since I personally come from the Christian tradition, I will focus on the implications for Christians.

It would be possible to put forward an argument that in a book of this kind, or in any academic endeavor, one should treat all religious traditions in what is sometimes called an "objective" fashion, standing outside all of them and treating all alike. On this basis, we should deal with the Christian tradition just as one might with the Buddhist or Muslim, taking a single item in each case and endeavoring to set forth its meaning. I have felt that it will be much more rewarding if we together explore, instead, the more relevant and more searching question of what is involved, for our faith, in the recognition of the profundity of other people's faith. For I believe that there is a relation between anyone's own personal faith and his or her understanding of the religious life of others. I believe that each is relevant to the other, and that it ought to be relevant. Our objective, I submit, is not to try to make these personal considerations irrelevant, but rather to understand the relevance, to criticize it and to purify and to use it. In other words, interreligious understanding is not merely an intellectual or academic or "objective" question; it is also a religious question. To ask about others' faith (or professed lack of it) is in itself to raise important issues about one's own.

The fact of my being Christian is relevant to my understanding the faith of Hindus, Buddhists, Muslims, and the like – the fact of my being Christian, and the quality of it, the question of what kind of Christian I am, and what kind I ought to be. Relevant similarly to your understanding are the questions of whether you are Christian or Jewish or sceptic, and if so what kind of Christian or Jew or sceptic you are. We can then turn to the theological and moral question of what attitude we ought properly to have, all of us, to each other; and to others across the world.

If one really insists on symmetry here, then I may concede that actually if I were publishing these thoughts in India (and in fact I have done something along that line), I would in that case present the Christian tradition in a brief introduction, I would omit the chapters that I have given here for the Hindu and Islamic traditions, and I would include instead of these a discussion of the religious implications for Hindus or Muslims of the fact that they hold their faith in a religiously plural world. (In India these days it is a profoundly poignant question; at least politically, although one could say that the political issues are consequences of inner attitudes.)

In other words, an ideally complete picture of our subject, flexibly valid for the whole world, would include two sets of issues: first, an exposition of each form of faith as it looks, or can at its best look, to an outsider; second, a consideration, from within each such form, of the fact of humankind's religious diversity, and its internal implications for that tradition.

Because I am writing in the West, I have chosen to do the expository presentation only for the traditions less familiar in that particular sector of the world. In this chapter, I intend to talk a little in general, but chiefly as a participant in the Christian tradition about the internal implications for that one group. Yet I am hoping that others among my readers may be able to recognize that this apparent partiality is superficial only. Ideally the intellectually valid goal is not some cold and impersonal "objectivity," but a self-development that is honest and leads to action.

Let us look, then, at three ways in which my being a member of the Christian Church is involved in my awareness of others' faith, and *vice versa*. We may call these three ways respectively that of personal experience, that of theological doctrine, and that of moral imperative. All three, we shall observe, are dynamic.

In the matter of personal experience, there is first of all the quite straightforward point that all learning is related to previous understanding, and is an extension of it. When I learn that Muslims worship God, or fear a Day of Judgment, or affirm Creation, and so on, then my capacity to grasp what they are talking about is obviously related in part to my own prior notion of what these terms mean – and to my experience that even in one community they have meant a variety of things to differing people and to different centuries, and indeed to the same person at different times in his or her life. Similarly a reader's capacity to understand what a Muslim feels and thinks and experiences in his or her orientation to God turns in part on that reader's own feeling, and thinking, and experiencing. If one is an atheist or indifferent, if the idea of God leaves one totally cold or one finds it repulsive, then it will be quite an extraordinary feat of sympathetic imagination if one can nonetheless enter validly into the experience of the Muslim; whereas those of us whose immediate awareness of God's presence (as theists put it) is vivid can much more readily appreciate what devout Muslims are talking about when they speak of living in that presence also. I am supposing here, of course, that we are not curtailed from this appreciation by some dogmatic bond that inhibits us from extending our awareness to other people. I will come to this question presently, under our second heading of doctrinal considerations. For the moment, I am simply asserting the basic point that my capacity to apprehend significantly the understanding of other religious persons turns in part on the religious understanding that I bring to it: my own ability to see more in life than its material or tangible forms, my own faith in moral and spiritual realities, my own sense of the divine – in a word, my own faith formed and nurtured in the Christian tradition.

Having said that, and emphasized it, I must nevertheless go on at once to recognize a few subtleties that complicate this situation. In a sense they are obvious enough, but the final implications are certainly subtle. I said that these things are dynamic, and certainly we are pushed into deeper and deeper waters by any serious consideration here. We are never left to stand still with any simple solution; rather each person finds him- or herself being led further and further into – into what? I was going to say "mystery," but only the religious among you will understand what I mean. Into transcendence? That term, too, may be puzzling. Let us simply say that the further one explores, the more one discovers there is to explore. This is part, of course, of what religious life is all about.

The first of the aforementioned subtleties is that, besides similarities, there are also, naturally, differences. The first step that Christians must take if they are to understand Muslims is to recognize that when the Muslim speaks of "God" or "Judgment" or "Creation" or the like, he or she is talking about the same matters as those to which a Christian also refers. (It is surprising how many Christians have not yet taken this first step.) Yet the second step is to discover that the Muslim is talking and thinking about them in a different way. Just how different, it is curiously difficult to say. All scholars are aware of divergences, certainly, but there is much less agreement among those scholars than one might suppose, as to just what those divergences are. It so happens that some of my own writings over the course of my life have been attempts to clarify more precisely than has been done previously the areas of correlation and lack of correlation between especially Christian and Muslim religious ideas. There is certainly a task of gradually coming to recognize how persons in differing traditions see things similarly, and another task of gradually coming to recognize how they see things differently. Both similarities and differences turn out to be other than one usually begins by supposing, or than has been traditionally taught.

Yet there is another subtlety here. First, I believe in God. A Muslim believes in God. This brings us together. Secondly, my idea of God and a Muslim's idea of God differ. This sets us apart again. Yet thirdly, I from my Christian upbringing and development know that God is greater – much greater – than my idea of Him/Her/It. The Muslim, as a Muslim, knows that God is greater – much greater – than his or her idea of Him/It. Does this bring us together again? It may, and it may not; that depends on many things, chiefly on that Muslim and on me – and on what kind of Christian I am, or have become, and on what kind of Muslim he or she is, or has become; and on what each of us does about it, and so on, and so on. As I said, this affair is not static but dynamic; it is not theoretic but personal.

I have spoken of the Islamic case, because at the immediate or basic level the similarities there with the Judaeo-Christian are clearest – though it does not follow that the ultimate liaison there is strongest. Let us turn to a more conspicuous example of divergence at the basic level – say with China. I have tried, by using the *yin-yang* symbol, to show that a person who in our sense does not believe in God may nonetheless have a faith in the universe that I personally recognize as comparable in part to Christians' faith in God. Ultimately, the concept "God" also is a symbol. It is one that in the West, also elsewhere, is used religiously. Yet not all religious persons use it. I do not know how successful I have been in leading you to recognize how it may be possible for Chinese to see a reality that I would call (though they would not) a divine quality in the universe, without their conceptualizing this in theistic terms. It is possible for them to see this, and for their symbols to nourish their capacity to see a facet of this reality (none of us sees more than facets); to have faith, and to grow in faith. Apart from the Chinese, there are many others to whom this applies, including in the West many secularists (some of whom have faith in reason, not, they say, faith in God).[18]

This applies also to many Buddhists, especially Southern Buddhists, for instance in Sri Lanka, for several of whom the concept "God," which they hear as alien, seems offensive.

Now I claim that I am able to grasp and appreciate these people's insights here – not easily, certainly, because it took me a long while to arrive at this, but eventually – because I, too, see this quality in the universe; and I have been led to see it by having been brought up Christian. Those of you who have also seen it in the Chinese symbol may have seen it for the first time there; but I should rather guess that most of you would have managed to grasp what I was talking about, and what the Chinese were thinking and feeling, if you yourselves had already come, through a prior faith of your own, to this awareness of ultimate harmony and reliability and beauty in things.

One of the things needed in a comparative study of religion is an ability to see and feel what theists call the divine, which ability I call faith (and what some Westerners nowadays call spirituality). Also needed is an ability to see it in new and different ways.

This brings us to one further subtlety; which is that learning a different, strange way of seeing something familiar can sometimes mean seeing it more clearly, more deeply. I have argued that insight here involves the religious capacity that one brings to it. It may involve also a heightened religious capacity which one may bring away from it. Again, we are in dynamism. All true religious life is a process, of the enlarging and strengthening of one's faith, one's spiritual depth. From my Christian start, I have spent my life finding more and more depth, greater and greater riches, in my Christian faith, and in other people's forms of faith. Or, let me put this more accurately: in God, to use the theist term, or in transcendence, to use the more general term.

For in that *yang-yin* symbol I hoped to show you not only something that Chinese see in the universe, but something that is actually there. The truth, if truth it be, is not in the symbol, but in the universe itself. The symbol merely expresses it (and nurtures it). If there is any truth in the Buddhist tradition, then its truth is not in "Buddhism," it is in the nature of things. The Buddhist tradition simply calls attention to it. It may call more or less successfully, and I from a Christian perspective may see it, or I may not; but if I do see it, and if it really is true, then I see it as a member of the Christian tradition, and rejoice. If anything at all is true, then it is part of God – the God whom I, as Christian, worship. Truth is God. I have already been introduced to God in my Christian faith. To be introduced is probably the most profound matter in anyone's life; the most crucial. Yet it is not enough to have been only introduced; and my Christian life has consisted in my allowing God to make more and more of that introduction, turning it from the incipient involvement that it once was into the richer involvement that it is today, and the still richer affair that, I hope, He/She/It may help it become tomorrow. My faith in God is nourished through many things – the equations of Einstein, the music of Beethoven, the death of my friend, the surge of the sea at dawn, Sunday services at my church, the history of India, the theology of Aquinas, the theology of Ramanuja. By seeing these matters in faith, I have seen them more truly, more richly, than I otherwise would have done. Yet also, by my seeing them, my faith becomes more true, more rich, than it would otherwise be.

The same applies to my study of others' faith. I may illustrate the point from my study of the Muslim mystics. While studying the Persian language I was introduced to the

Persian mystical poets, whose work happens to be some of
the most magnificent lyric poetry the human race has produced, and also some of the most superb expressions of
mysticism. I found it immensely exciting, relevant, revealing. By reading these Muslim poets, I learned a great deal
not only about the world, but also about God, and about
myself. I also came to understand for the first time the mystical strand in the Christian Church, which until then had
been a closed book to me. You may feel that it was perverse
of me to go this roundabout way to learn something that
was in my own tradition all along. Maybe. Yet the fact is
that I did. It may be urged that I need not, or even that I
ought not, to have learned religious truth from others that
I could have learned at home. My own view, and that of my
more charitable Christian friends, is simply to be glad that
I did learn it, and that my Christian faith is now that much
deeper, richer, truer.

Perhaps it will be interesting to add, too, that it was
from my study of Hindus, and of the Taoists of China, that
I have learned most clearly the limitations and dangers of
mysticism. Or to take an example from the other side of the
issue, my Calvinist background has certainly helped me to
understand and appreciate the more rigid Islamic theologians; but in turn, my study of these has illuminated for me,
and helped me greatly to understand, the conservative
Christian thinker Karl Barth, the power of whose position I
have only lately come to appreciate.

It may be objected that other Christians have understood and appreciated Barth without having been led to
that understanding and appreciation by orientalist routes.
Of course this is true, and proves the very point that I am
trying to make; namely, that one may arrive at an understanding of truth by various paths. This includes

"Christian" truths. The influence on contemporary Christian theology of the modern Jewish thinker Martin Buber is also relevant here.

We come now to the second of my three levels at which one's own faith is relevant to one's understanding of other people's. This is the theological. The situation is less happy here, but also simpler.

At the first level, that of personal experience, I have naturally drawn my illustrations from the Christian orbit, not the Jewish or Confucian or any other, but those of you who come from a different tradition can readily enough make your own applications. Somewhat the same applies at this second level, in the theological realm, though perhaps not quite so readily. In any case, I will speak of Christian theology. The fact is, as many of you know, that the dominant tradition in Christian theology has tended to take the line that the faith of other groups is, without further discussion, false. In other religious traditions outside the Christian, or outside the early Jewish and Christian traditions, humanity has been seen as seeking God, which we human beings are incapable of doing successfully on our own, while only in this one tradition does one have God seeking humanity, revealing and giving Himself (as in English the tradition phrased it). In this view religious truth and true faith were exclusively here. This has not been the only Christian position; from the time of the early Church Fathers, most notably Clement of Alexandria, and ever since, a more liberal strand has been developed. However, the exclusivist one has, certainly, tended to dominate.

This obviously is relevant to the question of a Christian's coming to understand the faith of others. For example, if university students of religion take this exclusivist theological current seriously, then they come to the task prejudiced, in the literal sense of having decided what they are going to find before having begun to study. Sometimes they have made this decision very firmly indeed, even to the disastrous point of feeling their own faith threatened if they find the faith of others more valid and deeper than the theologians had told them it would be. The theological problem is serious – let there be no doubt about that. But here, too, the situation is dynamic; struggle is involved. The truth may lie in the future, not in the past.

The important point here is to grasp what theology is. Theology is not faith; it is the attempt on the part of the theologian, who is quite human, to give an intellectual statement for his or her or the Church's faith. As Archbishop Temple[19] put it, theology is to faith as programme notes are to music.

My own view here is basically quite simple; namely, that the Church has as yet produced remarkably few satisfactory theological positions in the field of relations with other communities.[20] Christian theories of comparative religion have hardly been adequately worked out. In the Church in earlier centuries, the task was attempted chiefly by men who simply did not know, and certainly did not understand, the faith of the other great religious traditions of humankind. To be quite frank, they often just did not know what they were talking about. A revision of their views is therefore necessary. I affirm, with serious conviction, that a new and truer Christian theology in this matter is today needed, and is today possible – a theology that will be truer, more truly Christian. I am also reasonably confident that it will, in fact, be forthcoming – though whether it will be widely adopted is another question.

One simple point: on the whole there has been a tendency to hold that, the Christian faith being true, it must follow logically that other faiths are therefore false. This logic is simply not cogent. It has done great mischief, but it will not survive much longer.

The fallacy stems from confusing faith with theology, in one or other of its various forms. Since the conclusion conflicts with the faith itself, I infer that the theology used as premise must misrepresent its own master. I predict that a time will come, perhaps fairly soon, when Christians will see rather that if the Christian revelation is valid, then it follows from this very fact that the faith of others is valid too, is the form through which, equally, God enters their lives.

This is not the place to develop this argument. It is a large and serious business to elaborate a theological system that will do justice simultaneously to Christians' faith and to the fact that there are other forms that humanity has built to express its faith, forms through which successive generations have then found faith. It is the task of those of us who have seen and felt these two to construct such an intellectual position; or to enable others in the Church to see them, so that they may develop it. This much I can say: that although there is within the Church the strong traditional bias against such an interpretation, there is also within it today a much greater readiness for such a lead than I, at least, used to imagine. My own experience, in a few attempts to put forward something in this connection, has been that a great many Christians are waiting for newness here; that they would like to combine with their Christian faith an appreciation of outsiders' faiths, though they do not know quite how to do it. I do not here plunge into the theological argument; I simply insist that the problem is there, and is important.

Finally there is the third level of interrelation, which is the moral one. It is a major misfortune that this has at times been given less consideration than the theological. Certainly it is no less important, and no less relevant. In fact, moral considerations are relevant to theology itself. It is the clear moral imperative within Christian faith that I, personally, see as providing the basis for a revised theological position, which I advocated a moment ago.

For there is no question but that morally the Christian imperative is towards concord, fellowship, reconciliation, and love. The starting point of Christian theology has been the recognition of God in Christ. From this, two orders of inference flow: one at the intellectual level, of ideas and concepts; one at the moral level, of personal relations and action. Christians have tended to construct their systems of ideas, their theological doctrines, in such a way as to dig a great cosmic gulf between themselves and others – the saved and the damned. When we "Christians" have acted in terms of this dichotomy, we have at times fallen into such appalling crimes as anti-Semitism, apartheid, and the whole sorry business of color prejudice and Western arrogance towards the outsider. (It is the last of these that has provoked the profound resentments of anti-colonialism, and the current and widely under-appreciated anti-Westernism.) Morally, on the other hand, our ideal has been to bridge gulfs, not to dig them. We have been told to approach all persons with humility, to serve them, to treat them in love and with unfailing respect, to strive for harmony, equality, and a universal fellowship. When Christians have acted in this spirit, they have done some commendable and important things.

As I see it, this conflict between theology and ethics has never been resolved. If one had to choose, I personally would choose the moral dimension of Christian faith; for I feel that of the two, it is the more truly Christian. Yet I am a theologian, and am not willing to acquiesce in there being a conflict. I feel that the Church must strive to formulate a doctrinal position with regard to those of other forms of faith that will do more justice to our original revelation, and be more consonant with its own moral implications.

That, however, is in a sense an internal Christian question. Whatever you may think of it, there is still the point that the faith of other groups involves Christians morally in two ways. First, we are morally impelled, by being Christian, to try to appreciate that faith. Let us not fool ourselves into thinking that we can love a Hindu or a Muslim if we refuse to take seriously what is their most precious possession, their faith. Some have suggested that it is not Christian to be as sympathetic to those of other forms of faith as I have tried to be in these essays. I would contend rather that it is not Christian to be unsympathetic (though the Church has regularly been so). Others might disdain the faith of those outside their own group, but a Christian has no business doing so.

Secondly, we are morally impelled, by being Christian, to strive to construct a world of reconciliation and peace, of mutual understanding and global community, of universal human dignity. This means that it is our job as Christians to promote goodwill among religious communities; to create concord across religious diversity, to bridge the gulfs that so desperately separate people of differing faith. If one is honest, to accept human fellowship as an ideal is to accept, and to work for, a fellowship not of a we–they sort, but one in which some of *us* are Hindus, some of *us* are Buddhists, some of *us* are Muslims, some of *us* are Jews, some of *us* are Christians.

Let me close this chapter with some remarks addressed to readers who are not Christians. It was indicated at the beginning that our topic here was to be one's own and one's group's involvement in the lives and hopes and fears of fellow human beings; and particularly in their faith. I also indicated at that point that I would approach this general issue illustratively from the specifically Christian case. What about the Jewish perspective, however, or the Buddhist? What about the position of secularists? In one sense, clearly it would be presumptuous of me to speak of implications for Jews or others (except partially for secularists) as I have for Christians. Yet on this moral level I do have something to say, which is both all that I have a right to say, and all that I need to say. It is this. As I have tried to elaborate, a Christian ought to feel that the Christian community, as Christian, is obligated by the moral imperative of its faith to strive for understanding and love among all. Some Christians might go so far as to hold that they as Christians have greater cause, and greater resources, to strive for this than does any other group. Those of you who are Jewish or Taoist or whatever will hardly be disposed to agree with this. In your case it is your Jewish faith, or your Taoist faith, or whatever, that is your reason for so striving. Let us not quarrel as to which of us has the truer push towards universal brotherhood and sisterhood. We from the Christian side at least have too much for which we must ask to be forgiven. If any of us in any community believes that that community is the one to bring peace on earth, let them not argue the point but silently work to demonstrate this in practice.

What a marvellous new day would have dawned, if the only rivalry among religious communities were a competition as to which could make the greatest contribution to mutual concord!

My own aspiration would be that we should not compete in this but learn, somehow, to collaborate in it.

Conclusion

In this chapter I want to stand back and in some fashion consider the total picture. Can we ask: what emerges from the fact of humankind's religious diversity itself? What inferences in general may one draw?

One possible way to go at this sort of question would be the intellectualist or theoretical, addressing oneself to such important issues as how to conceptualize faith itself, in the light of its multiformity: not the faith of this group or that, but religious faith in general. How can one characterize this variegated human faith, what sort of quality in us can it be said to be, in a way that will do justice to our own and also to others' faith? Attempts at definition have been made in the past, by philosophers of religion and by theologians, and also by other observers more externalist, in fields such as sociology and psychology; yet often these proffered definitions have been on the basis of only limited material, chiefly that of one particular tradition, or alternatively with what some of us who do have faith feel is only limited insight into the quality of what it is in which we are involved. There is, I think, a legitimate and serious task here for the comparative religionist: to formulate ideas that attempt to do justice to both the profundity and the diversity – in the hopes of constructing theories that would prove acceptable both to Jews and to Buddhists, both to Muslims and to Christians, as well as being cogent within the academic tradition. This is an exciting and important endeavor; a pioneering one, because it is only in its infancy, but promising.

I myself have developed certain views in this realm, and I wondered for a time whether the function of this chapter might be for me to air them; but I have decided against this. My chief concern is not to push my own views but to take the opportunity to insist that the problems are significant – and soluble; and to urge more people to take them up. The theoretical aspect of these studies is important. We need more university departments, more books, more minds at work in this area of inquiry, more research, more scholarship, more creative thinking.

There is a still more persuasive reason for moving ahead. It is the vivid recognition that the question is not only theoretical and intellectualist. The massive dimension of the issue is the historical, the practical; and it is about this that I wish to speak now. We need new ideas, certainly, that will allow us to live in this new phase of human history into which we are moving, without blundering in bewildered confusion or narrow blindness. Yet rather than discuss the ideas that might serve, let us give our attention rather to the actual facts of our modern situation. In the emerging condition of our life on earth, not only new ideas but a new will and a constructive effort are demanded of us. It is not the failure to solve the problem theoretically that threatens us, so much as a failure to recognize that the problem is there, and is serious. The basic question of comparative religion in the modern world is not solely an intellectual question, requiring some neat theoretical formula – those of us who are theoreticians can handle that, at least if enough good minds will join in the search. No; the basic question here is an historical one and is a question for all – large, urgent, and deeply involving us every one. It is a matter most of all for our political leaders to guide us; but for all of us to participate.

I call it an historical question because it is a matter of what is actually going on in our century in world affairs, and of the direction in which civilization is going to move, and of our response to entering a new phase of human history. It is a question of our recognizing new trends and new goals, and of our constructing over the next hundred years (or so?) the religious aspect of a new kind of world that alone can now be viable.

The title of this chapter is "Conclusion;" but I hope that none of you will have taken that too seriously. For the religious life of humanity is not yet over. Indeed there are some facets of it that in a sense are just beginning, at least on a world scale – the very facets that most concern us here. Whatever one may think regarding one's own system, it is conspicuously clear to every discerning observer that the religious traditions of other people, and also of one's own community, are manifestly in continuing development. Even more striking is that the relations among religious groups are today in profound and even rapid evolution. The total religious history of the world is entering a new phase. For one thing, it is a rather new development that persons should be seriously asked to understand a religious tradition other than their own. What will develop when this becomes general it would be interesting to be able to predict. More radical, it is a new thing that people should be asked to participate in the processes of a religious tradition other than their own; and yet today it is hardly too fanciful to hold that our one-worldedness is bringing all humanity together in such a way that every one of us is being caught up in the processes of all. We must learn to work together, all of us, in jointly constructing and jointly operating the kind of world that all of us can jointly judge to be worthwhile.

As we all know, human development has reached a point where we must construct some kind of world order, or we perish. And humanness being what it is, this world order must have intellectual and moral dimensions, as well as economic and political. Our vision and our loyalties, as well as our aircraft, must circle the globe.

The West, by and large, has not yet seen this problem, and hence is proving, to a serious degree, inept in its attempts so far towards world leadership. Westerners usually assume without question that the new world order that is struggling to be born will in its essentials be of a Western pattern, will or even shall conform to our presuppositions, our norms, our notions of what can be taken for granted. We must wake up to the fact that the restlessness and drive of Afro-Asian "anti-colonialism" is not merely a rejection of Western political domination, but also and increasingly a refusal to think in Western terms. We must learn to share a planet, in ever more intimate collaboration, with those who judge differently from us, who value differently, who presuppose differently – in a word, with those of a different form of faith.

Some of you will perhaps say that surely we can get on with the business of political structures, of economic planning, of technical advance, of strategic defence, without raising "extraneous" issues of religious faith or cultural convictions: issues that may be interesting in themselves, but are irrelevant to secular concerns. This division of life into two spheres, religious and secular, is a characteristically Western pattern. We tend to assume that everyone else will share it, or if they have not done so in the past then they will "of course" learn it as they become modern. This is what I mean when I speak of our assuming that other people are like us, or that they will or must become like us tomorrow: that the problem of building a new world order is that of imposing Western civilization on the world. This is resented, and it will not work.

People of other civilizations have not only found or cast their faith in a different form from ours. They have also related that form, their religious tradition, to their civilization differently from us. Not only does religious faith vary, but the role of religious faith in society varies in various civilizations. I have often been struck by the fact that Western culture has two fundamental sources, which it has never entirely fused: one from Greece and Rome, one from Palestine. These two traditions have sometimes been in conflict, sometimes in harmony; sometimes one has tended to dominate, sometimes the other; often the two have intertwined; but they have never coalesced. Westerners each have two loyalties: one to their religious faith; the other to their secular heritage with all its range from politics and law to grammar. In the Western world, accordingly, what the West calls "religion" is seen as one factor in the total civilization.

In this matter, Western culture is unusual. In some cases one might almost say that Westerners have two faiths: their religious faith, and a faith in democracy, or in their national society, or even in their civilization itself. This last appears particularly in the special Western, Greek-derived, interpretation of rationality; and in the peculiarly Western idea of secularism, based as it is on the idiosyncratic Western concept of religion. In the case of China, India, and Islam, religious faith has not in anything like so neat a fashion been something separable from the rest of the social and cultural pattern. Although I would not like to try to define the matter precisely in a sentence or two, nonetheless one might perhaps suggest that it has not been one factor along with other factors such as the economic, the political, and so on, as in our society. It is not one element in a civilization; rather, it has been the form of that civilization. Ideally, it has been the pattern of whatever meaning the other factors in social life have. Thus in some ways one could perhaps say that it is the Western way of life that is our counterpart. This, too, is not one item in our social life; it is the form in which the items cohere. Rather than speaking of Hinduism, Buddhism, and the like, one should speak, and think, of the Indian way of life, the Chinese way of life, in South-East Asia the Buddhist way of life, and so on, as counterparts to the Western way of life. At the same time the faith of these persons is the counterpart also, of course, of our religious faith; and the greatness of their cultural achievements in the past has had to do with their ability to integrate these two.

Now the significance of all this for our purposes here is this. Most people in the East are not willing to set aside, or to leave out of consideration, their religious and cultural values, the form and pattern of their faith, in their resurgence in the modern world. To them, freedom and independence, which they have struggled so hard to achieve and are just now beginning to enjoy, mean in part an opportunity to reaffirm their religious and cultural traditions, to rehabilitate and revitalize and carry forward their respective ways of life. This means that the new world community towards which we hope to be moving must be a world community that includes and affirms reactivated Buddhist, Hindu, and Islamic religious traditions.

What is the West going to do about this? Its first task, I would suggest, is to recognize that the question of what it is going to do about it is significant, and must be answered. In the past, civilizations have lived either in isolation from each other, or in conflict with each other. It is a novel demand that they should learn to collaborate. None of us has learned it yet; the trouble in the West is that we have hardly even recognized that we have to learn it. There has been some recognition, though belated and partial, that the nineteenth-century solution of Western domination by force must be abandoned. And there has begun to be a retreat from the arrogance of cultural superiority. But a constructive recognition that we positively want cultural cooperation is a step that the West has yet to take.

I have argued that the Christian Church, for instance, will have to revise its theological assertion that would divide humankind into two groups: ourselves who are saved and the rest of the world who are damned. This is an immense demand to make upon the Church, but I make it. I make an equally large demand upon our secularist society, and am somewhat less confident that it will rise to the challenge, will have the courage and vision and faith to respond. For almost equally inadequate has been the uncultural or anti-cultural attitude, of so-called "realism," widely adopted in the modern West, that would disregard other people's faith (thought of in the West as religious faith, thereby excluding its cultural, political, economic, legal aspects), and would take into serious account only material things or "secular" matters. This view is pretty well embodied in official Western policy, which spends much time and energy and money on economic assistance, but pays virtually no attention to intangibles –

not by inadvertence, but by deliberate policy. In the Orient the charge is widespread, and ironically enough is fostered also by the Communists, that the West is materialistic, that we have nothing to offer but technology; that we are aware of and are concerned with differences in standards of living but not differences in cultural orientation, in philosophies, in faith; that we are fundamentally uninterested in how other people feel and how they think and what they cherish.

In other words, the Orient until now has been approached by the West chiefly on two levels – a religious level, on which the official Christian view has been that the beliefs and values of the Orient are wrong; and a secular level, in which the official view has been, and remains today, that their beliefs and values do not matter.

The fact is that, to the men and women concerned, these beliefs and values matter a very great deal – and matter also to the rest of us. These convictions matter not only in the sense that those who hold them, cherish them, regarding them as supremely precious. More subtly and elementally, they think by means of them, feel in terms of them, and act by them, and for them, and through them – even when they are thinking, feeling, and acting in the matters that we regard as political and economic.

It is my hope that these essays have helped, of course only in a minor and very introductory way, but still it is my hope that they may have helped to enable readers to see men, women and children of other faith as genuine persons, with genuine faith. For that, of course, is what they are: men and women like ourselves, who see the universe that we see, but see it in different ways; and who are our neighbours. A plea to understand them as persons, then, is a plea to learn who it is with whom we are now to cooperate, with what sort of men and women we are called upon now to build jointly a jointly satisfactory world. The first step, not yet seriously taken, is to recognize that we have to learn. We have assumed far too glibly that in our relations with Afro-Asia all we have to do is to give and to teach. The Canadian government in the Colombo Plan spends fifty million dollars a year in economic assistance and technical training. When it is suggested that along with this we should spend at least half of one per cent of all such amounts on cultural interchange, so far this idea has not only not been accepted, it has not been understood – it is thought of as a frill if not a distraction, rather than as a serious and even necessary move in international affairs.

A person of faith is one whose vision goes beyond the immediate environment, but whose life is lived within it; so that his or her task, as a person of faith, is to apply that vision to the immediate environment, in all its specific actuality. The problem of the economic development of a country like Pakistan, to take one example, is partly a technical problem in economics, and is partly a moral question of Pakistanis working at, and in, that economic development with the aspiration and courage and commitment – the sense of meaning in life – that are questions of faith. One cannot turn a poor country into a prosperous one without dams and steel mills and hydro-electric power; but neither can one turn a poor country into a prosperous one without getting up early in the morning, and passing up bribes, and throwing oneself into the task of implementing a vision whose benefits will accrue perhaps to posterity but not to oneself; without a loyalty to one's community and a commitment to its ideals that involve one's sense of life's meaning. Pakistan will not flourish if its citizens do not feel that life has meaning. If for them it does have meaning, then their name for that meaning is Islam.

The civilizations of the Orient are resurgent, in a new self-affirmation; and aim at a rehabilitation of their own traditions – modernized, creative, perhaps transformed, but still their own. It is their faith that life is worth living in the new and open world of today and tomorrow in the form of modernity interpreted in terms that they can understand and find good. Like us, they may fail before the challenge of modern technology, with its perplexing threat to the human spirit; or like us they may succeed. But if they do succeed, it will be in continuity from their own past, in their own self-interpretation.

The kind of world in which they and others will have managed to succeed, if they do, is one of multicultural values, of religious pluralism in tight collaboration.

I return to my question: what is the West going to do about this? There is absolutely no hope for Western leadership in the coming phase of world history unless the West can provide leadership towards that kind of world goal. Unfortunately, we have not begun to do this. Indeed, what we have begun to do gives the impression all too often that we are leading away from it. Basically, Western policy vis-à-vis the Orient, and Africa, and South America, seems to be postulated on an attempt to contrive ways of winning these people and nations over "to our side." Therefore we seem to them a threat to their own cultures, their own faith.

We should not ask other men, women and children to line up on our side, but we should contrive to let them see that we are on their side, or rather, that it is not a matter of sides at all; to let them see, and feel, that they and we are alongside each other, facing the world and its problems together. This means that we must be striving to build a world in which their way of life will flourish. The West must realize that a global defence against conflict and war is not a defence of "our" way of life, the Western, and not even a defence of "freedom" in the abstract; rather, it is a defence of the Western way of life and of the Islamic way of life, and of the Indian way of life, and the Buddhist way of life, and so on.

Any individual, any government, any movement that aspires to leadership in the world today must come to understand and to appreciate others' problems and aspirations, their convictions and hopes; and must attain a point of obviously wishing to see those problems solved as well as one's own, and to see those other cultures as well as one's own survive and flourish. Only with a West that believes Oriental civilizations worth defending, and Oriental dreams worth realizing, will the Orient in general be willing to cooperate.

The new world that is waiting to be born is a world of cultural pluralism, of diverse faith. No wonder we cannot bring it to birth as long as we have not recognized this, and have not deliberately and joyously set our face in this direction.

For there are two aspects of this problem of bringing to birth tomorrow's world. One is this that we have just discussed: that of recognizing the kind of world that it will be. The other is that of willing that kind of community. Western leadership may come eventually to recognize, through the failure of other approaches, that one cannot buy friends, and cannot even make friends with persons or communities if one disdains or ignores what those persons or those communities most deeply cherish or most instinctively presume, what they take for granted and what they reach out towards. However, even a radical shift in policy to take more seriously the human side of our relations with others will not succeed if it is done insincerely, on a purely utilitarian kind of thinking that we must pretend to have more interest in Buddhist art or Hindu philosophy or Islamic law if we are to work together with those to whom these things are precious – as a kind of more subtle method of winning them over to our side. Insincerity can cause as much resentment as disregard or disparagement. We must genuinely be on their side, not merely pretend to be. We cannot join with them in the defence of their ways of life unless we make it clear that we feel – and that means, unless we actually do feel – that those ways of life are worth defending, and are included in our long-range purpose. This was part of what I meant in saying that the problems of comparative religion involve not only an appreciation of others' faith, but also a widening and deepening of one's own.

Let no one imagine that building the new world community will be easy. Let no one imagine, either, that it must make room for the faith of Hindus, Buddhists, Muslims, and others, but not make room for ours. Christian faith and Jewish faith, and even Western secularist faith must be included in building that new world. So far as we are concerned here, all these are needed as foundations of it, and as foundations of our willingness, indeed our drive, to bring it into being. Nothing less will suffice. As I said about the *yin-yang* symbol, the truth at which we are aiming must not be bought at the price of sacrificing our own loyalties, our own tradition. At such a price it would not be true, apart from the fact that at such a price there would not be men and women to build it. We must move forward, not back. We must envisage other people of faith moving forward, not back. It is a creative task that is demanded of us all, not a destructive one of sloughing off any part of each group's vision that other people do not share.

Is this possible? Can such a variegated and yet harmonious world community be constructed? And can the individuals be found to construct it, by starting where they now are, each with their own faith?

I do not know. Theoretically, I am profoundly convinced that it is possible. Whether it is practically possible, in the perhaps short time within which we must achieve it, I do not know. This is a fundamental challenge facing humanity today; whether we shall rise to it or not remains to be seen. My own faith is that it can be achieved, and is worth achieving; and while I do not know whether we will rise to it, it is my faith that we can rise to it. This is all that practically matters, for a person for whom such a faith is vivid. Because our faith in it, and in the God who gives it validity, is fresh and simple, we are not discouraged by the possibility of failure, but rather excited by the possibility and need of success.

This excitement is real, and on that note I will close. I have spoken of these issues in comparative religion as problems, and of the tasks of envisaging and striving for a community in diversity as difficult and involving also problems. Perhaps the word "problem" was ill-chosen. They certainly are that in the sense that our best minds will only with difficulty unravel the intricacies intellectually, and only our best endeavors will carry us forward in practice. Nonetheless, certainly one should not speak as though the difficulties were depressing, or the massive nature of the practical task were anything but an exhilarating challenge.

I have tried to delineate something of the dimensions of the task, and something of its immense importance. To be caught up in a large and important movement, pioneering, historically crucial, with vast new issues at stake, involving the highest ideals of all humankind through history on the one hand, and the most delicate, realistic, and practical international problems today on the other – all this is stirring. Those who are reaching for the stars these days in the literal sense are, surely, launched on an exciting endeavor; but a metaphorical reaching for the stars that is involved in this quest for world community is more exciting, more significant, more rewarding.

Part Two

Part One of this book, above, is based on a series of radio talks which were then published as the first edition of this book. One of the talks, included also in this present edition as the chapter *"Implications for Oneself and One's Own Community"*, used the Christian instance illustratively as an example of the general point that relevant to the faith of any one community, or person, is the faith (and, to some degree, the thinking, the doing) of us all. The entire series, including that chapter, was addressed to any who might be interested in the overall topic. This brief second part here – also published in that first edition – is, on the other hand, a slightly updated and revised version of a lecture presented before an audience of Christian scholars; and deals again with the Christian case, but this time in a rather different way. As its title here indicates, it is directed especially to Christians, as an explicit challenge to modify their traditional thinking in such a way as to deal more adequately with the comparative question.

The Church in a Religiously Plural World

It has long been a platitude to insist that we live in a time of transition. There is excitement and at times almost terror in the new world in which even the cherished aspects of our past are giving way. Some Christians have hardly recognized that this dynamic, however commonplace in general, applies also to the Church's theology; and they may thereby include themselves among those for whom it means terror. Excitement comes rather when we become conscious that in fact the Church, existing as it does within history, has throughout been an institution in change and development; has always, consciously or unwittingly, spent each day on its way between what it was yesterday and what it would become tomorrow. We may rejoice in the new awareness that we, and indeed all other religious groups on earth, are and always have been participants in a process, not carriers of a pattern.

Such awareness involves also responsibility, particularly of course for those who are in any way leaders, fashioners for good or ill of the next phase of the on-going process: the clergy, theologians, biblical scholars, thinking laity, and so on.

I wish here to attempt to discern and to delineate something, at least, of a momentous current that has begun to flow around and through the Christian Church. It is a current that is about to become a flood, one that could sweep us quite away unless we can through greatly increased consciousness of its force and direction learn to swim in its mighty surge.

One of the transformations that we all face is the recent emergence of a new cosmopolitanism, permeating more and more areas of modern life. Widely noticed, thought about, and acted on, have been the political and economic aspects of our "one world." For Christians specifically this broadening means, according to the wording of my title, the Christian Church in a religiously plural world – which of course is the only world there is. To come to terms with living in it, however, especially with living in it gracefully, means for the Church a transformation.

Wrestling with the issues began at the frontier, on the "mission field;" the active confrontation of the Church with humanity's other forms of faith, other religious traditions. It was not long before it became evident that the concerns raised could not be left "out there" in the distance. Participants in those traditions, living by those forms of faith, have been increasingly present in the West, within "Christendom;" and the issues penetrate back into the scholar's study, pursuing us into what we were brought up to think of as the most intimate and most sanctified recesses of our theological traditions.

Regarding the missionary movement itself, except for fundamentalists who want no transition beyond what they know from the recent past, it is manifestly in profound crisis. Even the one-time acknowledged leader of the conservative wing of Christian missionary thinking, Hendrik Kraemer, closely familiar especially with missions to Muslims, affirmed that all attitudes on this matter "in so far as they are derived from the past, are therefore necessarily outmoded," and "betray . . . deafness to the voice of the sweeping turn in world-history and blindness to . . . the new situation." The religious history of humankind is indeed taking as monumental a turn in our century as is the political or economic history, if only we could see it. The upsurge of a vibrant and self-assertive new religious orientation among Buddhists, Hindus, Muslims, and others evinces a new phase not merely in the history of those particular traditions, but in the history of the whole complex of human religiousness, of which the Christian is a part, and an increasingly participant part.

A traditional relation of the Christian Church to the world's other religious traditions has been that of proselytizing evangelism, at least in theory. The end of that phase is the beginning of a new period, in which the relation of the Church to those of other forms of faith will be new. But what it will be, in theory or practice, has yet to be worked out – not by the Church alone, but by the Church in its involvement with these others.

The most vivid and most masterly summing up of the missionary crisis was perhaps the brief remark of Canon Max Warren, sensitive and responsible recent General Secretary in London of the Church Missionary Society. His obituary on traditional mission policy and practice was summed up in three sentences: "We have marched around alien Jerichos the requisite number of times. We have sounded the trumpets. And the walls have not collapsed."[21]

We turn from these matters to present-day theology, this chapter's central concern. Traditional missions are the extrapolation of an earlier theology of the Church. The passing of traditional missions is a supersession of one phase of that theology. The so-called "ecumenical" movements in the Western Church have been in part the result of pressures from the mission field because there, to sensitive missionaries, the problem of a divided Christendom "at home" came most starkly to light. It was from the mission field also that a fundamental fallacy in traditional theology has been shown up, though more recently as we have said it has been made the more vivid by the new pluralist situation in the West itself. The rise of science in the nineteenth century induced a revision in Christian theology – what has sometimes been called the second Reformation. Some may think that Canon Warren exaggerated, but at least he called attention to the seriousness of the new challenge, when he said that the impact of agnostic science will turn out to have been as child's play compared to the challenge to Christian theology of the faith of others.

The woeful thing is that the meeting of that challenge has hardly seriously begun.

The matter is illustrated by the career of probably the most widely respected Protestant theologian of the twentieth century, Paul Tillich. Towards the end of his life, in his late seventies, Tillich was invited to Japan, where his eyes were opened to a new horizon, and after his return he published shortly before his death a booklet comprising four lectures on *Christianity and the Encounter of the World Religions*.[22] Previously, however, during practically his entire productive and highly influential life, he had taught, and written works on, theology – understood as Christian theology, and as seen in its Western ambience.

A year or so before the end of that pre-Japan period, an illuminating story was told me by a friend from Harvard, where Tillich was teaching at the time. Apparently a letter in the student paper, *The Harvard Crimson*, was able to show up as superficial in a particular case this eminent theologian's understanding of religious

traditions in Asia. Some perhaps found it not notably surprising that an undergraduate in the second half of this
century should know more on this matter than a major
Christian thinker. Until recently, certainly, it was not particularly expected that a man (it normally was) should
know much, or indeed anything, about the religious life
of other communities before undertaking to become a
spokesman for his own.

To me, however, the incident raised a significant
issue. Looking at the matter historically, one might perhaps put it thus: probably Tillich belonged throughout
most of his life to the last generation of theologians who
could formulate their conceptual system as religiously iso-
lationist. The era of religious isolationism is about to be as
much at an end as that of political and economic isolationism already is. A major theme of Tillich's exposition
had to do with a theology's deliberate aptness for the
intellectual context in which it appears: the correlation
technique, of question and answer. Yet that context as he
saw it was the mental climate of the Western world; and
he was speaking to it just at the end of its separatist tradition, just before it was being superseded by a new context, a climate modified radically by new breezes, or new
storms, blowing in from the other parts of the planet. The
new generation of the Church, unless it is content with a
ghetto, will live in a cosmopolitan environment, which
will make the work of even a Tillich appear parochial.

Ever since the impact of Greek philosophy on the
Church – or shall we say the forced discovery of Greek phi-
losophy by the Church – in the early centuries, every
Christian theology has been written in the light of it.
Whether various Christian thinkers rejected or accepted it,
modified or enriched it, they formulated their expositions

aware of it, and aware that their readers would read them in the light of it. No serious intellectual statement of Christian faith since that time has ignored this conceptual context.

Similarly, ever since the rise of science and the forced discovery of science by the Church, Christian doctrine has been written in the light of it. Formulator and reader are aware of this context, and no intellectual statement that ignores it can be fully serious.

I suggest that we have entered a comparable situation with regard to other religious traditions. The time will soon be with us when theologians who attempt to work out their position unaware that they do so as members of a world society in which other theologians, who are equally intelligent, equally devout, equally moral, are Hindus, Buddhists, Muslims, and others; unaware that their readers are likely perhaps to be Buddhists or to have Muslim husbands or Hindu colleagues – such theologians will be as out of date as is one who attempts to construct an intellectual position unaware that Aristotle and Kant have thought about the world, or unaware that the earth is a minor planet in a galaxy that is vast only by terrestrial standards. Philosophy and science have impinged so far on theological thought more effectively than has comparative religion, but this will not last.

It is not my purpose in this essay to suggest the new theological systems that the Church will in the new situation bring forth.[23] My task here is to delineate the problems that such a system must answer, to try to analyze the context within which future theological thought will inescapably be set.

One of my theme songs in comparative-religion study has been that human religious diversity poses an intellectual problem, a moral problem, and a theological problem. In the rest of this essay I will consider the situation under these three headings – with emphasis on the last two. By "intellectual" I mean at the academic level: the sheer challenge to the human mind to understand, when confronted as it is today with what appears at first to be the bewildering variety of our religious life. At this level we have had or are having our Copernican Revolution, but we have not yet met our Newton. By this I mean that we have discovered the facts of our earth's being one of the planets, but have not yet explained them. The pew, if not yet the pulpit, the undergraduate, if not yet the seminary professor, have begun to recognize not only that the Christian answers on humanity's ultimate quality and purpose are not the only answers, but even that the Christian questions are not the only questions. The awareness of multiformity is becoming vivid, and compelling.

Before Newton's day it was thought that we lived in a radically dichotomous universe: there was our earth, where things fell to the ground, and there were the heavens, where things went round in circles. These were two quite different realms, and one did not think of confusing or even much relating the two. A profoundly significant step was taken when people recognized that the apple and the moon are in much the same kind of motion. Newton's mind was able to conceive an interpretation – accepted now by all of us, but revolutionary at the time – that, without altering the fact that on earth things do fall to the ground and in the heavens things do go round in circles, saw both these facts as instances of a single kind of behavior. In the comparative-religion field, a comparable dichotomy is seen, but has as yet not been satisfactorily interpreted theoretically. It is observed that many groups have in the past seen "our" tradition (whichever it be) as faith, others' behavior as superstition, the two realms to be interpreted in quite unrelated ways, understood on separate principles. The Christian's faith has come down from God, the Buddhist's goes round in the circles of purely human aspiration; and so on. The intellectual challenge here is to make coherent sense, in a rational, integrated manner, of a wide range of apparently comparable and yet conspicuously diverse phenomena. And the academic world is closer to meeting this challenge than some theologians have noticed (though at first it turned to the simplistic solution that all religious views were false).

Certain Christians have even made the rather vigorous assertion that Christian faith is not one of "the religions of the world," that one misunderstands it if one attempts to see it in those terms. Most students of comparative religion have tended to pooh-pooh such a claim as unacceptable. I, perhaps surprisingly, take it very seriously indeed; but I discovered that the same applies to the other traditions also. Christian faith is not to be seen as a religion, one of the religions. But neither is the faith of Buddhists, Hindus, Muslims, or Andaman Islanders; and to think of it so is seriously to misunderstand and distort it. However, this is a large issue that I am currently writing a book about;[24] forgive me for introducing it here, though it seemed perhaps that the point might be illustrative. I believe there is no question but that modern inquiry is showing that the faith of others is not so different from ours as we were brought up to suppose. (Their "beliefs" may be; but that is a subsidiary matter.)

The intellectual problem, however, because of its essentially academic nature, we may leave aside now to pass on to the two issues from religious pluralism that are of moment to us professionally: to all Christians as Christians, and saliently to those of us who are charged to perceive conceptually and to formulate intellectually Christian faith as we ought to have it. These issues are what I have called the moral problem and the theological problem that religious diversity raises.

Religious diversity poses a moral problem because it disrupts community. It does so with new force in the modern world because divergent traditions that in the past did and could develop separately and insouciant of each other are today face to face; and, perhaps even more important and radical, are for the first time side by side. Different civilizations have in the past either ignored each other or fought each other; very occasionally in tiny ways perhaps they met each other. Today they not only meet but interpenetrate; they meet not only each other, but jointly meet joint problems, and must jointly try to solve them. They must collaborate. Perhaps the single most important challenge that humankind faces in our day is the need to turn our nascent world society into a world community.

This is not easy. In fact, the first effect of bringing diverse groups together, and particularly religiously diverse groups, is often conflict. This may be overt, or hidden. On the whole, as I have already remarked, I think that few Westerners, including Christians, have any inkling of how profound and bitter and massive, and also how much on the increase, is anti-Western feeling throughout the world; and in Africa and in Asia this is in many ways anti-Christian. Christian antagonism to outsiders is evident mostly in the realm of color – though in more subtle ways it vitiates many other relations. There is also plenty of religious strife among the non-Christian traditions – as was explosively demonstrated in the Hindu–Muslim massacres around the partition of India.

Humanity has yet to learn our new task of living together as partners in a world of religious and cultural plurality. The technological and economic aspects of "one world," of a humanity in process of global integration, are proceeding apace, and at the least are receiving the attention of many minds and influential groups (though too often with an eye to power or profit for the influential). The political aspects also are under active and constant consideration, even though success here is not as evident as one would wish. The ideological and cultural question of human cohesion, on the other hand, has received little attention, and relatively little progress can be reported; even though in the long run it may prove crucial, and is already basic to much else. Unless we can learn to understand and to be loyal to each other across religious frontiers, unless we can build a world in which people of markedly differing forms of faith can live together and work together, then the prospects for our planet's future are not bright.

My own view is that the task of constructing even that minimum degree of world fellowship that will be necessary for humanity to survive at all is far too great to be accomplished on any other than a religious basis. From no other source than faith, I believe, can human beings muster the energy, devotion, vision, resolve, the capacity to survive disappointment, that will be necessary – that *are* necessary – for this challenge. Cooperation among persons of diverse forms of religion is a moral imperative, even at the lowest level of social and political life. Some would agree that the world community must have a religious basis, conceding that a lasting and peaceful society cannot be built by a group of men and women who are ultimately divided religiously, who have come to no mutual appreciation and understanding; but would go on to hold that this is possible only if their own one tradition prevails. No doubt to some it would seem nice if all throughout the world were Roman Catholics, or Communists, or Muslims, or liberal universalists; or if all would agree that religion does not really matter, or that it should be kept a private affair. Apart, however, from those who find such a vision inherently less appealing, if not downright frightening, many others will agree that for the moment it seems in any case hardly likely. Coexistence, if not a final truth of human diversity, would seem at least an immediate necessity, and indeed, an immediate virtue.

If we must have rivalry among the religious communities of earth, might we not for the moment at least, as we remarked in our chapter on the Chinese above, rival each other in our determination and capacity to promote reconciliation. Christians, Muslims, Buddhists, secularists, each believe that only they are able to do this. Rather than arguing this point ideologically, let us strive in a friendly race to see which can implement it most effectively and vigorously in practice – each recognizing that any success of the other is to be applauded, not decried.

There is, then, this general moral level of the imperative towards community, which in some sense all people of goodwill share. We may move from that to the specifically Christian level. Here I have something very special to adduce. It is a thesis that I have been trying to develop for a couple of years now. The thesis essentially is this: that the emergence of the new world situation has brought to light a lack of integration in one area of Christian awareness, namely between the moral and the intellectual facets of our relations with others.

I begin with the affirmation that there are moral as well as conceptual implications of revealed truth. If Christians take seriously the revelation of God in Christ – if we really mean what we say when we affirm that his life, and his death on the cross, and his final triumph out of the very midst of self-sacrifice, embody the ultimate truth and power and glory of the universe – then two kinds of consequence follow, two orders of inference. On the moral level, there follows an imperative towards reconciliation, unity, harmony, and fellowship. At this level, all humanity is included: we strive to break down barriers, to bridge gulfs; we recognize all people everywhere as neighbors, as friends, as loved of God as we are. At this level, we do not become truly Christian until we have reached out towards a community that turns all humankind into one total "we."

On the other hand, there is another level, the intellectual, the order of ideas, where it is the business of those of us who are theologians to draw out concepts, to construct doctrines. At this level, the doctrines that most Christians have traditionally derived have tended to affirm a Christian exclusivism, a separation between those who believe and those who do not, a division of humanity into a "we" and a "they," a gulf between Christendom and the rest of the world: a gulf profound, ultimate, cosmic.

I shall come to the theological consideration of these theological ideas later. At the moment, I wish to consider the moral consequences of our theological ideas. Here my submission is that on this front the traditional doctrinal position of the Church has in fact militated against its traditional moral position, and has in fact encouraged Christians to approach others immorally. Christ has taught us humility, but we have approached them with arrogance.

I do not say this lightly. This charge of arrogance is a serious one. It is my observation over more than twenty years of study of the Orient, and a little now of Africa, that the fundamental flaw of Western civilization in its role in world history is arrogance, and that this has infected also the Christian Church. If you think that I am being reckless or unwarranted here, ask any Jew, or read between the lines of the works of modern African or Asian thinkers.

May I take for illustration a phrase, not unrepresentative, which was under discussion a few years ago by the United Church of Canada's commission on faith, and which ran as follows: "Without the particular knowledge of God in Jesus Christ, men do not really know God at all." Let us leave aside for the moment any question of whether or not this is true. We shall return to that presently. My point here is simply that, in any case, it is arrogant. At least, it becomes arrogant when one carries it out to the non-Western or non-Christian world. In the quiet of the study, it may be possible for the speculative mind to produce this kind of doctrine, provided that one keeps it purely bookish. But except at the cost of insensitivity or delinquency, it is morally not possible actually to go out into the world and say to devout, intelligent, fellow human beings: "We are saved and you are damned;" or, "We believe that we know God, and we are right; you believe that you know God, and you are altogether wrong."

This is deplorable from merely human standards. It is doubly so from Christian ones. Any position that antagonizes and alienates rather than reconciles, that is arrogant rather than humble, that promotes segregation rather than fellowship, that is unlovely, is *ipso facto* un-Christian.

There is a further point at which the traditional position seems to me morally un-Christian. From the notion that if Christianity is true, then other religions must be false (a notion whose logic I shall challenge later), it is possible to go on to the converse proposition: that if anyone else's faith turns out to be valid or adequate or divinely given, then it would follow that Christianity must be false – a form of logic that has, in fact, driven many from their own faith, and indeed from any faith at all. If one's chances of getting to Heaven – or to use a nowadays more acceptable metaphor, of coming into God's presence – are dependent upon other people's not getting there, then one becomes walled up within the quite intolerable position that the Christian has a vested interest in other people's damnation. It is shocking to admit it, but this actually takes place. When an observer comes back from Asia, or from a study of Asian religious traditions, and reports that, contrary to accepted theory, some Hindus and Buddhists and some Muslims lead a pious and moral life, and seem very near to God by any possible standard, so that, so far as one can see, in these particular cases at least, faith is as genuine as Christian faith, then presumably a Christian should be overjoyed, enthusiastically hopeful that this be true, even though he or she might be permitted a fear lest it might not be so. Instead, I have sometimes witnessed just the opposite: an emotional resistance to the news, persons hoping firmly that it is not so, though perhaps with a covert fear that it might be. Whatever the rights and wrongs of the situation theoretically, I submit that in practice this is just not Christian, and indeed is not tolerable. It will not do, to have a faith that can be undermined by God's saving one's neighbor; or to be afraid lest other persons turn out to be closer to God than one had been led to suppose.

Let us turn, finally, to the theological problem that the existence of the other religious communities of humankind poses for the Christian (and that today's new immediate and face-to-face awareness of their presence poses urgently). This problem began, in a compelling form, with the discovery of America by Europeans, and the concomitant discovery of people on this continent who therefore had been "out of reach of the Gospel." In theory the peoples of Africa and Asia could have heard the gospel story and could have believed it and "been saved." If they had not become Christian, this could be interpreted as due to their stubbornness, or to Christian lethargy in not evangelizing them, and so on. But with the discovery of North and South American peoples who had lived for fifteen centuries since Christ died, unable to be saved through faith in Him, some sensitive theologians were bewildered.

In our day a comparable problem is presented, and may be viewed in two ways. First, how does one account, theologically, for the fact of humanity's religious diversity? It seems not to cohere with Christians' traditional sense of a world under divine aegis. It seemed comparable, in a certain light, with another relentlessly nagging Christian question, that of how one accounts theologically for the imperfection, at times devastating imperfection, of a world supposedly under divine providence. Why is the world not closer to good than it observably is; or at least more tolerably close? This question has never, some would say, found a satisfying answer, even though Christian theologians have been much more conscious of the "problem of evil" (theodicy) than of that of religious pluralism.

Another way of viewing the latter difficulty is to phrase a question as to whether, or how far, or how, non-Christians are "saved," or know God. This has of late found a considerable number of attempted answers, though to my taste none of these is at all satisfactory.

I would simply like to suggest that from now on any serious intellectual statement of Christian faith must include, if it is to serve its purpose in the Church, some sort of doctrine of other religious ways. We explain the fact that the Milky Way is there by the doctrine of creation, but how do we explain the fact that the Bhagavad Gita is there?

One may venture to comment on one of the answers that have in fact been elicited by the issue of pluralism. It is the one that we have already mentioned: "Without the particular knowledge of God in Jesus Christ, men do not really know God at all." First, of course, one must recognize the point that this intellectualization stems from and attempts to affirm, in however skewed a fashion, the positive conviction of the Church that "in Christ God died for us men and our salvation," that "through faith in Him we are saved." In the new formulations to which we may look forward, this positive apprehension must be preserved. Yet in the negative proposition as framed in the sentence that we are considering, one may see a number of inescapable difficulties, and one may suppose that the force of these will come to be increasingly felt in coming decades. First, there is an epistemological difficulty. How could one possibly know?

If one asks how we know the Christian form of faith to be true, there are perhaps two kinds of answer. First, we ourselves have found in our lives, by accepting and interiorizing it and attempting to live in accordance with it, that Christian faith proves itself. We know it to be true because we have lived it. Secondly, one may answer that for now almost two thousand years the Church has proven it and found it so; hundreds of millions of people, of all kinds and in all circumstances and in many ages and many places, have staked their lives upon it, and have found it right. On the other hand, if one is asked how one knows the faith of people in other traditions to be false, one is rather stumped.

Most people who make this kind of statement do not in fact know much about the matter. Actually the only basis on which their position can and does rest is a logical inference. It seems to them a theoretical implication of what they themselves consider to be true, that other peoples' faith must be illusory. Personally, I think that this is to put far too much weight on logical implication. There have been innumerable illustrations of the human capacity for starting from some cogent theoretical position and then inferring from it logically something else that at the time seems persuasive but that in fact turns out on practical investigation not to hold. It is far too sweeping to condemn the great majority of humankind to lives of utter meaninglessness and perhaps to Hell, simply on the basis of what seems to some individuals the force of logic. Part of what the Western world has been doing for the last four or so centuries (since that alleged affair in Pisa) has been learning to get away from this kind of reliance on purely logical structures, totally untested by experience or by any other consideration. The damnation of my neighbor is too weighty a matter to rest on a syllogism.

Secondly, there is the problem of empirical observation. One cannot be anything but tentative here, of course, and inferential. Yet so far as actual observation goes, the evidence would seem overwhelming that in fact individual Buddhists, Hindus, Muslims, and others have known, and do know, God. I personally have friends from these communities whom it seems to me preposterous to think about in any other way. (If we do not have friends among these "other" communities, we should surely refrain from generalizations about them.)

This point, however, presumably need not be labored. The position set forth has obviously not been based, and does not claim to be based, upon empirical observation. If one insists on holding it, it must be held against the evidence of empirical observation. This can be done, as one writer earlier this century formulated it:

> The Gospel of Jesus Christ comes to us with a built-in prejudgment of all other faiths so that we know in advance of our study what we must ultimately conclude about them. They give meanings to life apart from that which God has given in the biblical story culminating with Jesus Christ, and they organize life outside the covenant community of Jesus Christ. Therefore, devoid of this saving knowledge and power of God, these faiths not only are unable to bring men to God, they actually lead men away from God and hold them captive from God. This definitive and blanket judgment . . . is not derived from our investigation of the religions but is given in the structure and content of Gospel faith itself.[25]

Again, a careful study by a neo-orthodox trainer of missionaries in Basel said that Islam, like other "foreign religions," is a "human attempt to win God for oneself . . . to catch Him and confine Him on the plane of one's own spiritual life . . . and for oneself to hold Him fast."[26] He knows this, he says explicitly, not from a study of Islam but before he begins that study, from his Christian premises; he knows it by revelation, and therefore he can disdain all human argument against it. The position seems thoroughly logical, and once one has walled oneself up within it, impregnable. Those of us who, after our study of Islam or of Indian or Chinese religion, and after our fellowship with Muslims and other personal friends, have come to know that these religious traditions are, rather, channels through which God does indeed come into touch with these men, women, children – what answer can we give?

One possible answer is that empirical knowledge does in the end have to be reckoned with, does in the end win out even over conviction that claims for itself the self-certification of revelation. We do not deny that upholders of this sort of position are recipients of revelation, genuinely; but we would maintain that the revelation itself is not propositional, and that their interpretation of whatever revelation they have received is their own, is human and fallible, is partial, and in this case is in some ways wrong. (God reveals Him/Her/It-self, and we may again cast this in Archbishop Temple's words, that theology is to revelation what programme notes are to music.[27]) In fact, we have been through all this before. A hundred years ago Christians argued that they knew by divine revelation that the earth was but six thousand years old and that evolution did not happen, and therefore any evidence that geologists or biologists might adduce to the contrary need not be taken seriously. A repentant Church still claims revelation but now admits that its former theology needed revision. In the twentieth century the evidence has been increasing that the faith of those in other religious communities is not so different from our own as we have often asserted it to be. It has forced some to abandon any faith in revelation at all, and will in general, I predict, force us rather to revise our theological formulations.

Finally, even on the level of internal Christian doctrine itself this "exclusivist" position, as it is called – excluding non-Christians from salvation – is theoretically problematic. For according to traditional Christian doctrine, there is not only one person in the Trinity, namely Christ, but three persons: God the Father, God the Son, and God the Holy Spirit. Is God not Creator? If so, then is "He" not "Father" of all, not to be known – however partially, inaccurately – in creation, nor in people's lives? Is the Holy Spirit totally absent from any history, including even the history of others' faith?

It has been contended that outside the Christian tradition people may know God in part, but cannot know God fully. This is undoubtedly valid, but the apparent implications are precarious. For one may well ask: Is it possible for Christians to know God fully? I personally do not see what it might mean to say that anyone, Christian or other, has a complete knowledge of God. This would certainly be untenable this side of the grave, at the very least. The finite cannot comprehend the infinite. (Moreover, Church history makes the argument's fallacy all too apparent.)

(In asking what one actually means when one speaks of knowledge of God, we may recall here the aphorism from a chapter in Part One above[28] about the only true atheist being he or she who loves no one and whom no one loves. To know God, to use that theistic language, is not an ability to pass an examination in theology.)

Christians know God only in part. Yet one part of their knowing has been, surely, the recognition that God does not leave any of us utterly outside the knowledge.

It is easier, of course, to demolish a theological position than to construct a better alternative one. The fallacy of relentless exclusivism is becoming more obvious than is the right way of reconciling a truly Christian charity and perceptivity with doctrinal adequacy. On this matter I personally have a number of views, but the one about which I feel most strongly is that this matter is important – while the rest of my particular views on it are not necessarily so. In other words, I am much more concerned to stress the fact that the Church must work, and work vigorously, and work on a large scale, in order to construct an adequate doctrine in this realm, than I am concerned to push my own particular suggestions. Most of all I would emphasize that whether or not my particular construction seems inadequate, the position formulated above from which I strongly dissent must in any case be seen to be inadequate also.

Having expressed this caution, I may nonetheless make one or two suggestions. First, I rather feel that the final doctrine on this matter might run along the lines of Christians' affirming that a Buddhist who is "saved," or a Hindu or a Muslim or whoever, is saved, and is saved only, because God is (in part) the kind of God that Jesus Christ has revealed. This is not exclusivist; indeed, it coheres, I feel, with the points that I have made above in dissenting from exclusivism. If Christian revelation were not true, then it might be possible to imagine that God would allow Hindus to worship Him/Her/It, or Muslims to obey the One whom they perceive God to be, or Buddhists to act compassionately towards other "sentient beings," without responding, without reaching out to embrace them. Even, however, in traditional Christian language, because God is what He is, because He is what Christ has shown Him to be, therefore others do live in His presence. Also, therefore we (as Christians) know this to be so.

I rather wonder whether the fundamental difficulty in the formulated position here criticized, and in all similar statements, does not arise somehow from an anthropocentric emphasis that it surreptitiously implies. To focus on persons' knowing of God is to be in danger of moving in the realm of thinking of religion as a human quest, and of knowledge of God as if it were a human attainment, or even a human achievement. Of course it does not state it thus, but it skirts close to implying somehow that we are saved by *our* doings (or knowings). Must one not rather take the Christian doctrine of grace more seriously? The question must be more adequately phrased – in traditional language: Does God let Himself be known only to those to whom He has let Himself be known explicitly through Christ? Does God love only those who respond to Him in this tradition?

We are not saved by our knowledge; we are not saved by our being members of the Church; we are not saved by anything of *our* doing. We are saved rather by what alone could possibly save us, the anguish and the love of God. While we have no final way of knowing with assurance how God deals or acts in other people's lives (nor indeed in our own), and therefore cannot make any final pronouncement (such as the formulator of the position stated has attempted to make), nonetheless we must perhaps at least be hesitant in setting boundaries to that anguish and that love.

The God whom we have come to know, so far as we can sense the divine action, reaches out after all persons everywhere, and speaks to all who will listen. Both within and without the Church we listen all too dimly. Yet both within and without the Church, so far as we can see, God does somehow enter human hearts.

Notes

1. German *Mensch*, as distinct from *Mann*; Greek *anthropos*, as distinct from *aner*; Arabic *insan*, as distinct from *rajul*; and so on.

2. As an historian, I have been bothered, but now am amused, when readers fail to recognize such historical developments in the meanings of words that they are reading, fail to realize what the words meant at the time that they were written. ("Manufactured" used to mean "made by hand," as those who know Latin will readily appreciate.)

3. Our chapter "Muslims" might seem to be an exception; but see note 14 below.

4. I have elsewhere remarked that one of the most important matters about any human being is whom he or she means when saying "we." In my case, I sometimes mean my wife and I, or the person with whom I am speaking and I, on up to the entire human race past and present.

5. As I have documented in my two works *Faith and Belief* and *Belief and History* which are being reissued along with this present volume under the new titles: *Faith and Belief: The Difference Between Them* and *Believing – An Historical Perspective*.

6. Theologians are those odd folk who imagine that the truth about God can be stated in prose, one might say. Some would add that poets may reach a cut above – yet even they only partially, of course, as they themselves would be the first to admit. This present work, and others that I (and others) have written, come under a comparable sort of stricture; I am sharply aware that this book, and all my views on faith, are neither adequate nor final.

7. It seems to me beyond question that when Muslims have spoken of *iman,* it is legitimate, even requisite, to render this in English as "faith" – in our universalist sense, generic not specific. (To translate even *al-iman,* classically, as "the faith" would be a misunderstanding. This is despite the fact that it could of course be argued that by *iman* or *al-iman* Muslims understand human faith as essentially in an Islamic form, as by "faith" Christians traditionally understood it in a Christian form. In both cases they saw this as the only form of faith there is. In the Islamic case, this is still true today in probably even more cases than among present-day Christians; although traditionally, *vice-versa,* the Sufi movement evinced a great many more exceptions than were to be found in the Christian case.

8. Note the differences not only between Catholic Christians and Protestant Christians, but between, on the one hand, the majority on each side of that gulf and, on the other, the Nobel Peace Prize women who stalwartly strove to mitigate the clash. Could one not say that these women demonstrated more Christian

faith, though not more of "the Christian faith," than the two warring parties? One must speak, anyway, of a different kind of faith. Also, each of the women surely had her own particular, personal, faith.

9. See note 5 above.

10. The defence of their singlemindedness offered by, for instance, theists is that their faith is God-given. They fail to see that this, though true, does not preclude their, or their group's, apprehension and pattern of expression of it being their own response; that other persons' and other groups' apprehensions and patterns of expressions may also be built on a God-given base, yet also, like their own, humanly interpreted.

11. Some will remember a recent book which was on the *New York Times* best-seller list for an impressive number of successive weeks: *The Care of Souls*, by Thomas More. It was written by a former Jesuit and was a work that would traditionally have been seen as obviously a religious essay. Yet it avoided mentioning "faith" or "religion." I myself am one of those who find "spiritual," "spirituality" in danger of being heard in a rather sentimental or vague sense – which helps to explain my risky decision to keep the historical word "faith."

12. For my sense of the meaning of "person" and an historical exposition of the Christian affirmation regarding persons and the personal, see my *Believing – An Historical Perspective* (Oxford:

Oneworld Publications, 1998), pp. 6 and 85 at note 24, along with that three-page note for an examination of the rise of the Western concept of "person."

13. Luke 14:26.

14. Pronouns pose a more involuted problem than most English-speaking persons recognize, as regards gender. In the singular, English has three genders (*he, she, it*), French has two (*il, elle*). Some languages – Persian, Chinese, and others – have but one. In the plural, English also has only one (*they*); French continues to have two (*ils, elles*); Greek, Latin, and others in the West continue to have three.The issue has of late become spectacular in English in referring to God. Many have come to feel that the traditional use of He, Him, His is not acceptable (although even these generally do not use "Goddess;" and are not accustomed to a capital "G" for this word even in, for instance, English references to, or translations of Sanskrit *Devi* for the Supreme conceived as feminine; or they may add the definite article, "The," or "the," "Goddess" or "goddess"). The custom has arisen of referring to God in English nowadays as "He/She," "His/Her," and such. I myself have strong reasons for choosing "Him/Her/It," rather. One reason is that I see God as love, as justice, and the like (in French, "love" – *l'amour* – is a masculine word, "justice" – *la justice* – a feminine one, while in English both are neuter). Additional reasons I have set forth in recent publications.

All this is by way of leading up to my use, in this one particular chapter on the Muslims, not of all three but of the masculine pronoun in my English to refer, as above, to God. In Persian, as we have remarked, and in Hindustani, there is no gender in the grammatical sense for pronouns; thus the problem does not arise. The specific matter under discussion at this point in our text is a situation in India where the language in formal use was Persian, and in informal use, Hindustani. Shah Jahan, who had this mosque built, and the architect being cited, who designed it, spoke Persian (the latter, probably both), and so for them the question was non-existent, relentless though that question has become for those of us using English.

Muslims around the world and over the past fourteen centuries have spoken many different languages. Yet the guiding background of their lives has, for all, been the Arabic Qur'an, especially in matters relating to God. (All matters relate to God, of course; one should say, all matters where the relation to God is explicitly articulated.) Arabic, like French, has grammatically two genders; we call one masculine, the other feminine (although virtually all nouns are grammatically "masculine" unless there is some formal or substantial reason for their being given a feminine form: the word for "person," whether male or female (*shaks*), is masculine; the word for "personality," whether of man or woman (*shaksiyah*) is feminine. The Qur'an explicitly, even vehemently rejects any notion that God should be thought of as feminine – as a goddess. It does not follow, however, that God should, or might, be thought of as masculine, as male. Such a notion is rejected almost as vehemently as its counterpart; and Muslims throughout have been not merely offended, but appalled, at what in their eyes is the anthropomorphism of

Christians conceiving of Jesus as a god, and of God as a "Father." A case therefore might be made that a pronoun in Arabic used in referring to God might be rendered in English, with its embarrassing discriminations, as "It;" but to many English-speaking Muslims this sounds deeply derogatory, as if God were a thing, were something less than we, instead of infinitely greater than we, and than all else.

The practice has arisen of Muslims using in English "He," "Him," "His;" and I have adopted this in the present chapter.

(An aside: the difference between "gender" – traditionally a grammatical matter – and sex is interestingly illustrated in for instance German, where the words (*sic*) for "girl" and "woman" (*das Mädchen, das Weib*) are neuter. In French, the word for "elephant" is masculine, so that a cow elephant is *un éléphant femel.* It is striking that in Arabic the adjective for "pregnant" (*hamil*) is in the "masculine" form, on the grounds that males cannot be pregnant and therefore there is no need to specify the feminine. Even in English, a ship is "she," and a gathering of persons is "it." It is not the case that the thoughts and feelings of everyone on earth can be neatly fitted into the patterns of the English language.)

15. For a study of the changing meaning over the centuries of the words "believe," "statement of belief," "believing," and their worldwide counterparts, see my *Faith and Belief: The Difference Between Them* (Oxford: Oneworld Publications, 1998), and my *Believing – An Historical Perspective*, (Oxford: Oneworld Publications, 1998).

16. See *Believing – An Historical Perspective*, chap. III, "The Bible: Belief as Non-scriptural," pp. [70]–99, and specifically p. 74.

17. James 2:19, based on the King James Authorized and Revised Standard versions.

18. I have developed in later publications the point that secularism, and especially secular-humanism, has at times been a form of faith. See, for instance, my "*Philosophia*, as One of the Religious Traditions of Humankind: the Greek legacy in Western civilization, viewed by a comparativist," in *Différences, valeurs, hiérarchie: textes offerts à Louis Dumont*, ed. Jean-Claude Galey (Paris: Editions de l'Ecole des Hautes Etudes en Sciences Sociales, 1984), pp. 253–79. (Maison des Sciences de l'Homme – Bibliothèque.) Also, most recently chap. 8 (sc. pp. 176–95), "The Classics," in my *What is Scripture? A comparative approach* (Minneapolis: Fortress; London: S.C.M. Press, 1993).

19. In his *Nature, Man, and God* (the Gifford Lectures for 1932–34) (London: Macmillan, 1935), p. 317.

20. Examples that come to mind are Nicolas of Cusa in the fifteenth century, and John Hick in the twentieth.

21. This and the quotation from Canon Warren given at the end of our next paragraph, are remarks made in an address at Scarborough, Ontario on 18 October 1958.

22. Paul Tillich, *Christianity and the Encounter of the World Religions* (New York: Columbia University Press, 1963).

23. Some twenty years after giving this lecture I took a preliminary step in this direction, in my *Towards a World Theology* (London: Macmillan; Philadelphia: Westminster, 1981; Maryknoll, New York: Orbis Books, 1989).

24. Subsequently completed and published as *The Meaning and End of Religion* (New York: Macmillan, 1963, and later editions, currently Minneapolis: Fortress Press, 1991).

25. Edmund Perry, *The Gospel in Dispute: the relation of Christian faith to other missionary religions* (New York: Doubleday, 1958), p. 83.

26. Emanuel Kellerhals, *Der Islam: seine Geschichte, seine Lehre, seine Wesen*, second edition (Basel and Stuttgart: n.p., 1956), pp. 15–16, translation mine.

27. Cf. p. 141 above.

28. Cf. p. 73 above.